Walking Out Of the Darkness,

Stepping Into the Light

Violet L Rose

ISBN-13: 978-1508832799

ISBN-10:150883279X

I dedicate my story to Mary Lu, my mom, sister, and husband thank you for being there for me.

Success can happen if you work hard for it!

By Lynn

Authors Notes

This book I am about to write is not set out to hurt anyone but to help others who are going through Multiple Personality Disorder and do not know it yet or may know it and do not know what to do about it. Multiple Personality Disorder, which is now currently being called, Dissociate Identity Disorder, is a disorder that is caused by severe ongoing trauma or abuse. Sometimes life deals you out a bad hand and you have to learn how to roll with the punches so to speak. However, in my experience with this gift as I am proud to call it and you will see why, I had to not only roll with the punches that life dealt to me, but I had to fight to just keep alive. The names of some of these amazing people have been altered to protect their identity.

I would like to take this time before moving on to thank the people that were a very big part in helping me through my fight for survival through my healing process. Without them, I would have never made it as far as I have in becoming as strong as I am right now. With their help, I am able to function normally, as can be expected. First, I want to thank my sister Jane who stood by my side and helped me deal with the green house and trailer, which I will be explaining later in my story. She let me be mad, get my rage out, and yet lovingly set boundaries so that I would not hurt myself or anyone else nearby. She dropped everything for me and because of her in one day, I made a major step in healing. There have been many times, she was there for me, but this one day was a big day for both of us.

Then there is my husband Bill. Of course, marriage is difficult at times but let us take into consideration the big picture of our marriage. He has stayed with me for all these years with all the switching and confusion I have done and helped me become more alert on how I acted and to keep focused on the big picture of which my actions would influence, our two kids. When I did not want to eat, he would remind me that our little girl was watching, and would I want her to think it was ok to act this way. He kept me thinking and to stay on track for them as well as for myself. Most marriages would have been destroyed do to the fact that living with someone that you never know who you are coming home to would be very hard to deal with every day. However, he has stood by me no matter what I did or who did it if you know what I mean.

The next person I want to thank is my mom Ann. She believed me when I told her what happened to me, when I was fourteen years old. When I told her what happened to me when I was five years old and when I had a problem or was troubled she dropped everything she was doing and listened to me and it did not matter that it was two or three in the morning.

When the alters became active she rolled with my switching and treated them accordingly. It did not matter if I acted like a two year old or a four year old or even when Pal who is eight asked her what she was to call her. My mom spoke to them, as they needed to be spoken to. She believed in all of my alters and gained their trust and they knew they had someone safe to go to whenever they needed to tell their story to someone.

She was gentle and kind to them. She welcomed any of them who wanted to sit on her lap or just talk. If you are a parent and you have a child with Multiple Personality Disorder if you get nothing else out of my story please at least keep in mind what my mom did for me and use her example on how to help your child.

Now there is however one more person that I want to

thank and that is my counselor Mary Lu. She did an awesome job with me and I will forever have her in my heart. She helped me see color and light in my mind once again. She helped me find all the alters and listened to their stories for five years. When I got off track in behaving myself, she helped me get back on track. It is because of her dedication to my healing I no longer have amnesia and am co-conscious. It is because of her I can remember and can tell my story.

Walking Out Of the Darkness, Stepping Into the Light

I was twenty-six years old and had my whole life
ahead of me, so everyone thought.
 I had a good job, and people from my religion that loved
me very much. I had friends who I thought cared for me
and cared about what happened to me. I had a wonderful
mom and sister and a family who loved me very much
and still do to this very day. Everyone thought I had it
together both mentally and physically. I was going to
college to become a Medical Assistant. I had the world
in the palm of my hands and a future that would mean
everlasting happiness.

My Grandpa Jones had just died March 6 1992
and I missed the good times we had when I was living
with him and I did not know in my mind if this was ok or
not. I did not want to go to his funeral. I was afraid to go.
You see he had abused me when I was a child and when
I was fourteen years old, my mom and I were reading an
article from a magazine, which stated that in an incest
situation the child is innocent, and that the abuser is
completely at fault. That the child is to tell anyone that

she/he felt safe with about the abuse. I yelled "NO!" threw the magazine across the room and ran to my bedroom. My mom quietly came in and sat by me on the edge of my bed.

"He lied to me" I said.

In a soft voice she asked, "Do you want to talk about it?"

"You would not believe me if I told you." I answered.

Again, in a calm voice she said, "Yes I would."

"Why would you?" I asked in defiance.

"Is it about Grandpa Jones?"

"Yes it is, how did you know?" I asked in surprise.

"Did he hurt you?" She asked in concern.

I told my mom about our little secrets that Grandpa told me that no one was to know about. He had made it clear that I was the bad girl if I told anyone about our "games."

She smiled at me and gently and said, "I believe you honey."

She assured me saying, "You are not a bad girl at

all. He was the bad one for making you play his games. God does not like the games that he played and God is not mad at you. He is mad at Grandpa."

With a shocked look on my face all I could say was, "Really?" She had shared with me that I was not alone in this nightmare. On this day, I felt that my mom saved me from Grandpas nasty games. I had learned from this magazine that he had lied to me all these years.

I became very scared and did not know why, because he was dead and he would not know that I had told anyone. Oh but guess what? He did know. I confronted him about what he did to me when he was on his deathbed when I was twenty-four years old. He asked me if I thought that my mom would ever forgive him. I jumped out of my chair and asked him, "What do you think? Look at what you did to her children. That is up to mom to forgive you or not." I told him that my mom knew for a very long time and asked him why he did this to me. He did not say much at this time. I asked him, was there anyone else that he had abused, and I found out that yes there was. He told me that I was the one that he abused the worst because I was around more than the others were. I asked him if anyone had ever abused him as a child. He admitted that he was as a young boy. I told him that people have said that when some people have been abused as young children that generally they become abusers themselves.

I made it very clear that the abuse had stopped with me. I reminded him that I am an aunt and I have been a nanny. I have never harmed a child, I never ever will, and to this day, I hold this promise to be true. He asked me if I would ever forgive him and I explained, that if I wanted God to forgive me for my sins and transgressions then I need to obey him and forgive people who have sinned against me. I also told him when he began talking about God forgiving him, "That wages through sin pays is death" and that he was on his way to pay.

After he had died, inside my mind, I became confused and had a lot of fear that came over me. I felt like I was losing my mind and I could not stop it. I was hearing voices that would say my name out of nowhere when I would walk down the hallway at work. I would look around to see who was there and found that I was standing there all alone. I was seeing a counselor trying to get a grip on my life that was slowly slipping away from me. I remember telling my mom, "I do not know why I am doing the things I am doing. I do not want to do them but I cannot stop it."

I ended up in the hospital for attempted suicide October of 1992. I was admitted into the psychiatric ward, which was on the fifth floor, the first two days in the hospital, I was on a fifteen-minute suicide watch twenty-four hours a day. I was angry about how my life had ended up. Soon after going through therapy I started to open up and began talking about my feelings and myself to other people that were in the hospital with me. My mom never missed a day to come see me. I found out real quick that my so-called friends were not my real friends. I had only one true friend nearby and that was my mom. She never faltered. No one else ever came to see me.

One day while my mom was visiting me, we were playing a card game. The nurse came in to give me my medication and asked,

"What game are you plying?"

11

My mom looked at me and said,

"Do not say it!"

I looked back to the nurse and politely said,

"We are playing crazy eights!"

We all laughed and the nurse stated that if I keep it up I would be going home very soon. It felt so good to laugh again; it had been a very long time that I had anything worth laughing about.

One evening one of the patients and I got bored and wanted to do something fun so I put nine Dixie cups in the middle of the hallway and took some apples and we went "Bowling." Whenever we hit them, we all would yell "STRIKE!" There came a time when I was allowed off floor privileges and one of the patients and I went down to the second floor, since the staff that worked in the other parts of the hospital were nervous to be around people like us I decided to mess with their nerves a little. Therefore, when we got onto the elevator I saw that the nurse that was already there had pushed number four button. I asked her in a weird tone "going up to the fifth floor?" with a strange smile on my face. The next thing I knew she was getting off on the third floor instead of the fourth floor. Oh well, go figure.

Now do not get me wrong, I am not making light of the reason why I was there and why everyone else was there, I was getting stronger and I had realized during my stay at the hospital that life was too short for me to take it away. In addition, what I did for the other patients was that I showed them the same thing and made them smile again.

Going Home

It was now November of 1992 and I went to my counselor who was seeing me before I went into the hospital. She noticed me switching and asked,

"Who else is here besides Lynn?"

A small voice from my twenty six-year-old body said "Pal!"

"Where is Pal now?" The counselor asked.

The small voice says, "Over there." As I pointed to the lamp that was off to my left side.

"How old are you Pal?" The Counselor asks.

The small child like voice says, "I'm eight years old."

"Whom else do you see Pal?" The counselor asks.

Pal stated, "I see a shadowy figure that lurks in the dark."

The counselor states, "We will call this one Shadow. Is there any more that you see?" The counselor asks.

Pal's answer was, "Yes. I see someone who is

really angry and he is very big in size."

"OK," the counselor says, "We will call this one Anger."

The counselor sees that what she has discovered here with this twenty six year old women is way out of her scope of practice and when I had shivered and was able to speak to the counselor with a clear mind, the counselor had told me of the four different alters she had discovered during our session. There was Pal, Shadow, Anger and Lynn the core personality.

The counselor tells my mom and me what she had discovered and that there was a lot of work to do and she suspects that what I have was known as, M.P.D, which means "Multiple Personality Disorder" my mom gently, said in a quite tone "No Wonder."

I asked my mom "what do you mean by that?"

She explained that one evening she remembered when I curled up in a ball in her lap while she was sitting in my Grandpa Don's rocking chair and talking in a childlike voice saying, "I don't mean to be bad Mamma, please help me! I'm so sick."

15

She also said, "I never knew whom I was coming home to from one day to the next when I came home from work."

I was never the same type of person as the day before. Can you just imagine? Here was this twenty six year old women sitting on her mom's lap rocking just like she use to when she was two or four years old. However, my mom bless her heart just patted me on the back and rocked me softly.

On Nov. 12, 1992, I met Mary Lu, I took what was called a DES test. Which is Dissociative Experiences Scale (DES)? It is a screening test for Dissociative Identity Disorder (DID) and I scored very high which could indicate that I indeed have Multiple Personality Disorder. Now maybe because of this test I will know why I did the things that I did and had no control in stopping them.

This is what Mary Lu puts in her first report. "Thinks she is a Multiple, has identified several alters including Pal who is eight, Shadow age unknown, and a third whose job seem to be punishing Pal."

Significant history: "From age five to ten

Grandfather abused her sexually. He said she was bad and this is why her dad had left her when she was four years old. He promised that he would never leave her and that she was his favorite. After a period, he very brutally tortured and killed her pet rooster Blackie and said that if she told anyone of their games he would do the same to her.

She has had counseling off and on once at eleven years old and again at seventeen years old for ill temperament and then for severe weight loss as a teenager. She was dis-fellowshipped from a religious congregation on Aug. 20, 1992 for conduct unbecoming of a Christian. She could return after a period of faithful church attendance and showing repentance. She is part Cherokee Indian and her Grandpa Jones gave her an Indian name. She had a dog she dearly loved that died Aug. 16, 1991 whom she still grieves over to this day. She now has a cat named that she has gown very fond of, that was born the same day her precious dog died.

Lynn wants to continue counseling once a week. Will encourage journaling and try to be acquainted with her system. Build in supports internally and strengthen

17

support from her mom, which seems good. Mom believes her and in fact moved away from Grandpa Jones because of having knowledge of his past behavior."

The week went by, my mom and I did some reading on the subject, and we both found out that I did have a great deal of the symptoms of having Multiple Personality Disorder. When I saw Mary Lu again, Nov. 19, 1992 she showed me my test score. The highest score on the test for Multiple Personality Disorder was 57.06. My score was 54.01. There was no doubt on Mary Lu's mind that I most certainly have Multiple Personality Disorder. I knew now that our work was going to be difficult for all of us in figuring out what made me tick and digging out my past. I found myself being in denial. There was an alter who kept stating that this was all made up and that I was making this up to just seek attention.

I believe that this was the first alter that Mary Lu spoke to. The denier stated, "This is not real. "We" have never heard of such a thing. "We" are just trying to get attention and make up excuses for "our" behavior. "We" are just making this up. It is nothing but an attention getter." Notice that this alter was speaking in third party. This is common when someone is disassociating from himself or herself. Yes indeed this was an alter speaking. For many months, the denier was not convinced that this was a real condition. So I began to educate myself on this matter.

Beings I was in a state of denial I also read a brochure that she gave me called "Switching Characteristics." This is what I found. "There are headaches," in my case, the headaches are on the right side of the base of my head.

"There is pressure inside the head; your neck feels stiff and pressure at the base of the head. Your pupils become dilated and there is pressure behind the eyes. There is blurred vision and then your vision becomes clear then blurry again, your eyes become watery or glossy, glazed in appearance. Your eyes can appear reddened and reddened eyes without memory symptoms mean that a part is functioning that has repressed material attached to it. Your eyes can become more sensitive to light. Many times, you can feel lightheadedness or dizziness. There could be chills and your ears start to ring. You could physically feel shorter than usual and or emotionally feel more child-like. Objects and people look different. Your body looks and feels detached and your face will look different in the mirror. Also your voice will change like a child or low or high tones." MDWeb, *better information, better health*, WebMD, LLC

These symptoms are just a few of what I found in myself. You may wonder how Multiple Personality Disorder develops. In another article Mary Lu gave to me, it explains it this way, "When faced with over whelming traumatic situations from which there is no physical escape, a child may report to "going away" in his or her head. Children typically use this ability as an extremely effective defense against acute physical and emotional pain, or anxious anticipation of that pain.

This dissocial process, thought, can separate off feeling, memories, and perception of the traumatic experiences psychologically, allowing the child to function as if the trauma had not occurred. Multiple Personality Disorder is often referred to as a highly creative survival technique, because it allows individuals enduring "hopeless" circumstances to preserve some areas of healthy functioning. Over time, however, for a child who has been repeatedly physically and sexually assaulted, defensive dissociation becomes reinforced and conditioned."

In my case, we found that as a baby, I nearly died of some unknown reason and it took Penicillin shots to save me. When I was born, I weighed 10 lbs. 6 oz. When I was 7 months old, I weighed 9 lbs. I had to have a shot every day for several weeks then one every other day and then the shots became less frequent over time. This was something good for me in the outcome but the pain was unbearable so we figured this is when I learned the gift even before the abusive destruction had begun. The article continues to mention, "Because the dissocial escape is so effective, children who are very practiced at it may automatically use it when they feel threatened or anxious-even if the anxiety-producing situation in not abusive.

Often even after the traumatic circumstances are long past, the leftover pattern of defensive dissociation remains. Chronic defensive dissociation may lead to serious dysfunction in work, social, and daily activities. Repeated dissociation may result in a series of separate entities, or mental stated, which might eventually take on identities, of their own. The entities may become the internal "personalities" of a Multiple Personality Disorder system. Changing between these states of consciousness is described as "switching."

People with Multiple Personality Disorder may experience any of the following:

"Depressions, mood swings, suicidal tendencies, sleep disorder (insomnia, night terrors, and sleepwalking), Panic attacks and phobias." I also experienced chest pains. These are commonly called panic attacks. Alcohol and drug abuse, also compulsions and rituals, psychotic-like symptoms (including auditory and visual hallucinations), also eating disorders. In addition, individuals with Multiple Personality Disorder can experience headaches, amnesia, time loss, trances, and "out of body experiences. Some people with Multiple Personality Disorder have a tendency toward self-persecution, self-sabotage and even violence (both self-inflicted and outwardly directed)." Buzzle.com by Nilesh Parekh

Great deal of these symptoms are in my case and in some cases not every one of these symptoms are experienced but a majority of them are and can or will cause someone with Multiple Personality Disorder who does not know it yet, to interfere with daily living or activities. It also can cause changes in behavior and cause a person to live a life they do not normally agree with. You find yourself living a life that you would never have thought of doing in your wildest dreams.

"Is Dissociative Identity Disorder Real? What Are the Symptoms of Dissociative Identity Disorder? What is the Difference between Dissociative Identity Disorder and Schizophrenia? What Roles Do the Different Personalities Play? Who Gets Dissociative Identity Disorder? How Is Dissociative Identity Disorder Diagnosed? How Common Is Dissociative Identity Disorder?" WebMD, http://www.webmd.com/mental-health/dissociative-identity-disorder-multiple-personality-disorder

It is very important to do research and become educated in knowing the truth regarding Dissociative Identity Disorder or formally known as Multiple Personality Disorder. To be able to help someone that may have this disorder you have to equip yourself in knowledge to be able to successfully recover or help someone who is struggling with the symptoms of this disorder.

Now the reason I ended up in the hospital was that I over dosed on my medication, drinking alcohol on top of it, and cutting up my wrist, I saw the blood and I called 911. I did not want to die. I just wanted this mass confusion to go away. The police officers showed up and saw I had the ice pick in my hand. The damage on my wrist was not too deep but it was a cry for help. I had a new kitten and he was my sweet friend, when the police came into the apartment my kitten sat up on the back of the couch where I was laying down and began to swat at them. He did not want these men near me. The officer took the ice pick from me and while using my phone to call in my condition, my kitten politely put his paw on the receiver and hung up the call for him. The officer was laughing at this two month old "guard kitten" and said, "It looks like someone really cares about you." My kitten kept interfering with his call and the officer just gently pushed him to the side until his call was over. I could not help but smile.

I arrived at the hospital with the officer and he called my mom to tell her what I did and where I was. Then he sat with me for a while.

I said, "You do not have to sit here with me. Take me home. I will be just fine. I did not want to die I just wanted this pain inside to go away."

He tells me a story stating, "The last time I was on one of these calls, I listened to the suicidal person and took her home as she requested. I believed her that she would be ok. An hour later, I got another call for the same house. When I got there, she had followed through and had killed herself. I will not make the same mistake with you. I want you to live a long life." I will always be grateful to that officer.

What turned me to get to this point? Feelings of despair, depression to the point of not eating even less than I already was. Feeling lost and alone, beings that someone I dearly cared for at the time left me and went to another person made me feel abandoned, thrown away and deserted, I had no one to be with or turn to. No one had time to listen to how I was feeling, accept for my mom. She was always there; she made it very clear that no matter what was going on inside my mind even though we did not have a clue at the time, she would always be there to see me through it.

I felt that no one cared accept for my mom and sister, and so why should I? I was very angry. I gave up so much of my life, and the things I had faith in for someone who I thought loved me, for what? To find out that him and those who I thought were my friends just turned their backs on me anyway.

While I was in the hospital, during therapy I noticed my vision was going blurry and that I could only see a hazy gray where ever I looked and then to find out that I was talking about some memories of a chicken. When we were supposed to be talking about depression and what led us to end up in the hospital. There were about six or seven of us in this counseling group.

I had memories of hearing a chicken cry out in pain and the next minute hearing a thunk and then total silence. The next thing I knew was a shiver that came over me, when my vision came back I saw that the whole group had their eyes glued to me as if they were watching a thriller movie. I felt weak and so tired, every muscle in my body ached and my neck and back felt so stiff as if I was sitting in one place for hours when in reality I was only sitting there for a half hour.

During my efforts to go to religious meetings, I found that the others were very scared to be there. Sewry age thirteen kept coming out because she saw Papa who was an Elder in the congregation; this is what she called him during this time. His real name was Jack, he meant so much to me as a child growing up in the congregation before anyone had any idea what was going on. I was dis-fellowshipped from the congregation because of immorality, before I was diagnosed with Multiple Personality Disorder.

During the meeting with the Elders, all I could talk about was hearing a chicken cry and then silence, and how afraid I was and that I did not know why I kept hearing this cry repeatedly. The Elders kept looking at me with confusion not knowing and neither did I at the time who was speaking to them. They kept trying to get me back on the subject of why there was a committee meeting and I would just go off track again about this chicken. This was the right thing to do beings it had appeared that I was unrepentant. The alter Sewry felt that Papa never forgave her for the bad things she had done. He told her that it was not up to him to forgive her but it

27

was up to God. That is very true but all Sewry wanted to hear was Papa saying, "I forgive you and I still love you." However, he never did.

I told Mary Lu, "I had another spell at the Kingdom Hall again this week and mom had a hard time getting me back. Pal was stubborn. The confusion of all the little ones was very strong. I ran in the back room and sat in one of the chairs. Someone came in. His name was Bob and he is one of the Elders. He was so nice to me. He went and got my mom and she came in and sat with me. Pal came out and asked what this man's name was and my mom says this is Bob and he cares for you very much."

Now keep in mind that I have known Bob for ten years, so you can only imagine what was going through his mind to hear someone that he knew for so long ask her mom what his name was.

The alter Pal who is eight years old continues to tell Mom "I am so scared because Grandpa knows I told you about our secrets and he is now going to hurt me just like he said he would when he killed Blackie."

My mom says" Grandpa is not here anymore. He

died and he cannot hurt you".

Meanwhile Bob is standing in front of us seeing all of this.

Pal started to feel better and asked Mom, "So he cannot get me?"

Mom says, "No Pal he will not get you, Bob and I will not let him even if he was still alive."

Sewry also remembered Grandpa Don, who was the good grandpa and she missed him very much. He died when I was thirteen years old and I felt that he never knew how much I truly loved him before he died. Sewry, who is thirteen years old, remembers the night he died and tells Mary Lu her story.

"He was in the hospital when he fell and broke his collar bone on Friday and no one took x-rays until the following Monday then it was too late, he ended up with pneumonia and Monday night he died because of that. Lynn was such a brat to him while he was living."

Sewry states to Mary Lu. "I did not even get the chance to say sorry, that I loved him so much, and to say thank you to him for being such a good grandpa to me. Mom says that to not worry, he always knew things even if she thought he did not."

Sewry switched back to adult Lynn. Mary Lu and I talked about Grandpa Don's death but on this day, I was unwilling to deal with it. We worked on my inside safe place. In the beginning, there was total darkness inside my mind. There was no color inside when I looked for it. It is like when someone asks you to close your eyes and picture a bright sunset and you really can see it when you try it. Close your eyes if you will. Picture a sunset. What colors can you see? Some say they see orange and red colors. Well I could not do that. In fact, I remember my mom telling me that when I was five years old in school I would color everything black. It never entered our minds of why I did this way back then until now. It was as if I was stuck in a black closet with no way out. I lived in my mind's eye in total darkness.

When a person with Multiple Personality Disorder, is ready to integrate the core personality or birth person has to be active. If the core personality is not active then the alters cannot integrate to become a complete person again. My core personality is very active so in time we hope that I will become complete again. This was a goal we all had, that is if Lynn would ever be ready or ever want to become complete again. I would have to find a way out of my darkness and live life in color. This will be very different for me because I have never experienced it before. A lot of work is still ahead of us and it will be a frightening journey for me.

My safe place is as beautiful as the Garden of Eden so I thought anyway. Mary Lu had me picture in my mind's eye some place where the little ones could go when they got scared of a memory. She helped me see light and color that I never saw before, so this was going to be hard. It is like asking a blind man what the color red looked like. If he never saw red before how would he be able to tell you? The same went for me. I have lived in what seemed like a closet type place in my mind my whole life that I could not comprehend what light and color would look like when closing my eyes. This how we did it.

Mary Lu had a wand with a red ball on one end of it and she would wave it in front of my eyes and have me picture something good that I would go to when I was a little girl. Note that this wand was not used as a tool for hypnosis. I would not allow hypnosis to be used on me. I did not believe in it and believed it would do more harm than good. It was used as a trigger to bring out the memories of my child hood that I had suppressed my whole life. I began to remember a weeping willow tree that was on my Grandpa Jones farm that I would climb up into and I remembered how good it felt to see out but no one could see me because of the willow branches that hung clear down to the ground. I use to climb this tree when I needed to hide from him when he wanted to play" his games." It was my hiding place from his abuse. Therefore, Mary Lu had me put this tree in my safe place.

Then she had me remember something good about my mom's dad, my Grandpa Don by waving the same wand that had a red ball on the top of it in front of my eyes. I began to see the ocean and the waves falling down onto my feet. When I was ten years old I met my Grandpa Don for the first time after my mom, my sister and I came back from Canon Beach. So now, there became an ocean off to the far left of my safe place. A cliff sits in the distance off to my right side where a waterfall runs down into the ocean. This waterfall could be a memory of the first waterfall I had ever seen during this same year and this waterfall was Multnomah Falls.

There is a stream of water where the alters go to wash off when the memories get to bad. Then off to the upper left corner of the cliff is a gravesite where the bad memories are buried once they have been dealt with in a healing way. The weeping willow tree sits near the bottom of the cliff and on the other side of the water stream is where the animals are grazing on the fresh grass. A memory chest sits right by the rocks at the right side of the bottom of the cliff. The birds sing and the animals play and this is where we go to stay safe. When a memory gets ruff we go under the weeping willow tree where we can see out but no one can see us.

There is a bright light that shines upon us when we become afraid and The Peace Maker, whom we discovered, sits in the light for the little ones to go to when they need peace and harmony. The Peace Maker dances with her Indian beauty shining in the bright warm light. There was color of the rainbow, which shines over the horizon at the end of the oceans lining where the sun sets every day. What I see is color, and it is the first time in twenty-six years.

When my German Shepard died, I had a very hard time dealing with her death. She was a gift from my sister Jane when she was one years old and was my best friend. She was fifteen years old when we had to put her to sleep in my arms. It was a painful loss for my mom, sister, and I beings she was such a big part of our lives. Mary Lu did some work with me inside my mind to help me deal with the loss of her. Then this inside work on my memory of precious dog triggered the memories of the day when I was informed that my Grandpa Jones died which in turn triggered a memory of my pet rooster Blackie who was killed when I was eight years old by my Grandpa Jones. Mary Lu discovered a twelve year old alter that looked like Lynn, and found that in my mind's eye, she loves to play with our sweet canine friend that we miss so much.

Pal my eight year old alter had this bad memory of Grandpa Jones, and she was so scared to remember how Blackie died. Mary Lu had Pal go to the stream to wash off the blood and to go to the safe place to be comforted in my mind's eye by The Peace Maker who is spiritual and who brings peace to all of the alters inside when they are scared, and tells Pal that it was not her fault. Grandpa was bad and not she. I was so scared to remember how Blackie died that I switch again to Sewry the thirteen year old alter.

Mary Lu put in her notes. "Lynn is initially tense and tired. Lynn did much weeping during abreaction. Lynn is calm at the end."

Mary Lu encouraged Sewry to write a letter to Grandpa Don telling him how much he meant to her and either burn it or take it to the ocean or to his gravesite, which ever was best for her.

The next session with Mary Lu my mom came with me. It seems that one night after I had gone out with some friends, someone came out to speak with my mom. I had a spell in which a two year old had come out at home. This little alter was discovered to be called Little Anger. Little Anger was in fear of Grandpa Jones and saying she was bad and had to hurt. Little Anger had a screwdriver, which she was using to scrap across my wrist. Then my mom heard her crying, she got up from her bed quietly, and says, "Who am I speaking to?"

This is when the child like voice says, "I'm Anger but I am only two years old." Mom asks Little Anger what she was doing with the screwdriver.

Little Anger points to her chest and says, "I hurt!" she says that she was bad and had to hurt.

The little alter says pointing to her chest, "hurt here" then points to the wrist she was cutting on.

"Pain, I need pain."

In Mary Lu's documents, she puts this, "Lynn is comprehending memory work. Lynn is also showing good control over parts of each story. She is catching on to how to be a good parent like person to the children who are inside her mind. We will continue with memory work

The Shadow That Lurks In the Dark

"I am Shadow!" A strong voice begins to speak to Mary Lu.

"I have been watching you. I do not come out very often. Lynn left yesterday. She was going to see a friend and he was not there. She felt so let down. It was as if she was not important to him. I feel the pain and confusion. I have to be strong. I am not afraid of her perpetrators any more. I can handle them. It is dark and lonely inside. We try to help one another. So much is missing."

There are two alters inside that starve the body. One uses starvation as a way of punishment, her name is Angie who is fifteen years old; the other starves because she thinks she is fat and feels it is a way of control. Her name is Annie and she is twenty-two years old. Throughout the years, I had a history of dating men that were manipulators. I allowed men to use me probably because I did not know any other way to get them to notice me. I felt that if I let them have their way with me they would not leave or hurt me physically. It is just as I felt with my Grandpa Jones.

Shadow continues to talk to Mary Lu, "Canopy picks losers and always wanted a canopy bed to feel loved in. She is the one who always seeks for love and never finds it. She has no sense."

Mary Lu documents this in Lynn's file. "Shadow is dressed in drab colors. She has her face down and looks away. She speaks in a quiet monotone. She appears sad and depressed. She seems to want to talk about current events today. Lynn and I are working on a teamwork system so Lynn can know what goes on at work in case someone has to take over for her. We are going to work on inner communication and develop a structure and containment for more intense memory work later."

I partied almost every night with so-called friends or just by myself. I drank a lot and did some hard drugs to get away from the voices in my head. I hung around with these people and the men I chose for companionship because of fear of being alone with these voices. These people are from a dysfunctional family as well as I was, and we discussed on ways to find more stable group of friends. We worked on my co-

consciousness and accepting responsibility for all my inner parts. A few of the alters smoke cigarettes and the others do not. I can recall one night when I was alone at home that one minute I was watching TV and the next minute someone bumped into my chair and a shiver came over me and I found myself drinking a beer and smoking a cigarette in a bar. An alter drove me to this bar and I did not even know it. Talk about being scared now! It was Shadow who drove me to the bar.

One time my sister went to Mary Lu with me to get a better understanding of what Multiple Personality Disorder was. I remember before my stay at the hospital, Jane sat me down at the kitchen table with my mom and asked,

"Why do you do what you are doing? You treat Mom as if she was the one dis-fellowshipped".

I remember telling her that I was so bad that I did not want Mom to get into trouble with the elders by speaking to me. My mom began to cry and told me that she would not get into any kind of trouble and that she loved me very much. You see when a parent has an ill child they are to take care of that child no matter how old the child is. This is the case with me, even when the child is dis-fellowshipped.

I began to cry and stated, "I do not know why I am doing the things that I am doing."

As the conversation continued, a chill came over me and my vision began to get blurry but I had no idea at this time what was going on. During my session with Mary Lu while Jane was with me, Jane got a better picture of what was going on. Our communication with each other got stronger and stronger. There was finally an answer for Jane on why her little sister acted the way she did. She is seven years older than I am and we are like night and day but now we have finally become close friends.

She stated, "Having this information on why Lynn is acting the way she has been for so many years, I can work with this. Now I can help her when she needs it. I am better equipped to seeing whom I am speaking to and how to find out if I am not sure who is out. Knowledge is power and I have more power to understand Lynn."

Knowledge and education of M.P.D was half the battle in being more patient and having a better understanding of my odd behavior.

The death of my Grandpa Don was very hard to get over because I felt that he left me without me saying, "I love you." To forgive your self is probably one of the hardest things that some people can do. I know this because I am one of them. Mary Lu and I discussed Grandpa Don's death and how I could help the other alters come to a forgiving conclusion about the day he died. I chose to go to his grave. I began to feel nauseated during the session. In my mind's eye, I went inside and saw Sewry. She would not talk. She was curled up in a ball. I was able to seal off the memory and bring her to The Peace Maker who took her to the stream of water that flowed from the waterfall into the ocean and dipped her in to feel clean and fresh. Then I took her to sit under the weeping willow tree.

This is what Mary Lu puts in her report. "Lynn is very resistant to internal work. Weight loss may be a serious issue. Having control is certainly a serious issue. Lynn will see her physician on Monday. We will discuss anti-depressants and need for hospitalization. If weight loss continues we will stop therapy and work on medical care."

My mom and I went to my Grandpa Don's grave one weekend. We sat by the grave. It was the first time I have been there since he died. My mom stated that where I was sitting is where we sat at his funeral. Then I began to cry very loudly and very strongly. I let out a lot of hurt on this special day. Then we went to the ocean in my safe place, and watched the waves roll in with the tide. Grandpa was a sailor when he was in the navy. So this had deep meaning to me that I could use for future healing from his death.

My mom said, "It's like he went out to sea on a voyage and that he will be back again someday."

It was March 17, 1980 when he died. I was thirteen years old. While I sat, by his grave I read my letter to him aloud telling him how much I loved him and that I was so sorry I did not tell him so every day that he was alive. This letter was for my own peace of mind. It was to help me heal and to stop living with regret.

One night while my mom was giving report to me at work where we worked together in a assisted living facility, I began to cry. I had switched to an alter named Little Anger. I had a memory of being left with a babysitter who scared me very much when I was two years old. In addition, when my mom left that night to go to work, Little Anger thought mom was leaving her. When we got home, my mom took me on to her lap and Little Anger began to feel safe again.

Little Anger says, "She looks like she is going to hurt me. I have nightmares of her beating me so badly that I see blood on the wall. (Which never happened but she scared me so badly I had the nightmare). She made very ugly faces at me and always seems mad at me. The other kids would go play and I had to stay behind and be around her. I was afraid to do anything for she might spank me."

I remember sitting on the porch and I looked behind me and there she was and she made this dreadful look on her face at me. Boy was I so scared! I would scream and cry for my mom every day when she dropped me off and all day when the babysitter was not looking. Jane told my mom about what was going on and my mom stopped working and went on Welfare to provide for us so that I did not have to see this babysitter any longer.

During my therapy with Mary Lu we discovered so far an alter name Bitter, who is sarcastic and uses harsh words at times. She is not as harmful as some of the other alters, however, she feels betrayed. There is one named the Quiet One, who is ten years old and sits by the weeping willow tree and rocks. She is a country girl like Pal. She was created when we moved to Portland Oregon. She will not talk to anyone. She just looks around and watches what everyone else is doing.

There is also Little Anger who we have already met who is two years old. She conflicts pain to the body as a way to express the pain she feels emotionally. Then Big Anger who is an adult and looks very strong like a male type figure and he yells when he is angry. When he begins to yell it is as if he verbally has gone crazy. He is mad at everyone and everything. He is verbally violent. There is Pal who is eight years old. She was created when my grandpa killed my pet chicken Blackie. She feels scared all the time, fidgets with her fingers, and is shaky. There is also Sewry who is thirteen years old. She misses my Grandpa Don who died when I was thirteen years old.

There is Angie who starves the body as a way of punishment. When I feel hunger pain, she feels it is a punishment and that the body deserves to be punished for the bad she feels she has done. In addition, there is Annie who thinks she is fat and starves the body because she feels very fat. She is anorexic. The less she weighs the better she feels about herself in addition to feeling in control. My life was going out of control and so Annie makes me feel in control of something such as if I gain weight or not.

There is Little Cheryl who is four years old. She helps me deal with my dad abandoning my mom, sister, and I when I was four years old. Big Cheryl is seven years old. Big Cheryl was created when my mom and dad got a divorce. There is Chameleon who talks with an accent or changes the way she talks according to her surroundings. During a night that Grandpa Jones was abusing me, I mentally went away to a faraway land where in my mind he could not hurt me anymore. I mentally went to Australia or England. Anywhere that he could not abuse me and play his games. Then there is Clown. I remember when I was very young and still lived on the farm, I would try to make my cousin Mae and her friends laugh. I was good at it too. The Clown is a teenager now and does not take anything very seriously. This was when I needed to get away from the pain inside, so I clowned around to see others smile. I even wanted to smile again and The Clown helps me do that.

Then of course, there was Canopy, which we have already met. She has brown hair and is pretty in her own way. She is not stuck up but is sort of flirty and bubbly. She looks for love and attention in any way she can find it. In addition, we must never forget Shadow! She wears black and a hood that covers up her head and face. She does not trust anyone and glares at everyone. She does not have any friends nor is friendly. Then we have No Name. She is very busy doing things and has to be on the go. She cannot seem to stay in one place for very long. She goes for walks or cleans house. She chooses to not be named. She feels having no name can keep her safe from harm. Having a name is too personal and does not want to be close to anyone. In addition, last but never least, Lynn the core personality. There we have it! The list gets bigger. What is more amazing? There is still more to be discovered! It takes many years for a person with D.I.D to discover their whole system. There is a lot of work to be done. It is not just the matter of discovering them, but it is the matter of them telling their stories and recovering from the nightmare, to work towards the ultimate goal and that is integrating.

During my therapy I was trying to go to college to be a Medical Assistant and I remember the times when one day I would do so well with word perfect and understand everything I was working on in school, then the next day or two I could not remember anything I had done the day before. We discovered that one of my alters was going to school while "Lynn" took a mental trip from reality. Shadow was a very good student. Too bad I was never around before the tests. I could not do my schoolwork, not only because of a knee injury but because I could not stay focused long enough to be able to finish the work. Therefore, I had to quit school half way through.

During one day with my mom when we were at the school and they were telling me that I had to go to school every day and then I had to work graveyard too, Little Anger came out and had a temper tantrum, stamping her feet and jumping up and down screaming "I do not want to go there!" Just imagine, seeing a twenty- six year old woman jumping up and down like-- well? Like a two year old, this is how old Little Anger is. It was funny looking to say the least. Beings that I was part co-conscious, I remember laughing at myself, and my mom laughing with me too.

Annie

Annie is one of my strong alters. She has a powerful mind of her own. Her story goes like this.

"I feel powerful when I control the body with food. My whole life has been having other people tell me what to do. I am very fat and I feel happiest when I stop eating and lose weight. Because I have the say so on weather I gain weight or not. It is all about control and I have it. I am tired of people hurting me and taking away my power. For the less I weigh the less people can hurt and abuse. People have hurt me so deeply and I will not allow it anymore. It is my life and no one else's. I am stubborn in what I do or not do. It is my choice not anyone else on losing the fat or not. When I lose weight, I forget what others have done to hurt me."

Angie loses weight as a form of punishment. To hurt the body because she feels the body deserves to hurt. She does not feel fat she just uses hunger as a punishment. As for me, I am fat there for I must lose the weight. If I do not succeed in losing the weigh then I am a failure in all things. Losing weight is all I know how to do and I do it

ANNIE

There is a lost soul I see within, she
roams around lost and confused, for her
frame is very thin.

It is food she will refuse, for the less she
weighs the less people can hurt and
abuse.

She was born with a heart of soft precious
gold; it was abused and taken; now it is very hard and
cold.

Her future seems so dark and bleak; it is
joy and happiness she yearns to see.

Where will she find it? This is unknown,
for she feels so frightened and all alone.

Her story is painful, she is afraid to tell,
for she knows if she does, the pain will be hell.

There is a lost soul that roams within, her
story is untold, and she refuses to give in.

To lose five pounds is hard and tough, but
those few pounds are never enough.

There is a story she hides deep inside, her
name is Annie, all she does is run and hide.

What will her future be? She will not let
us see. Only time will tell if we wait patiently.

May 8, 1994

As time went by I began to be more aware of my inside parts and was able to be co-conscious most of the time. I still had some moments of time loss but not as bad as in the beginning. I began to grow up and wanted to move away from my dysfunctional friends. There were times the Quiet One would come out in front of Mary Lu and it appeared she was very lonely. The Quiet One spoke to no one at all. She just sat there with nothing to say. It was as if she was in a state of a deep depression and in a zombie like state of mind. She seems to be very sedated looking. She does not want anyone to be around her and wants to be alone. If she does not talk then I do not know how she will be able to tell her story.

I guess I will have to look deep inside and try to help her through it. I was still extremely thin and this alarmed everyone inside, because if the body dies then everyone else would die too. I still had a problem of being very compulsive at times. My ability to make adult decisions became hard to do.

This is what Mary Lu put in her report. "Guided

imagery: Feels a maze inside and keeps running into barriers. When asked what would help, she started to cry and said, "Go back to my faith!"

Mary Lu continues to write, "Somewhat arrogant at first. She appears to continue to lose weight; softly weeping as the eating disorder is her way of gaining control. She does not appear very healthy at this point. She is aware of danger but afraid to eat for now. Her physician is aware of this eating problem and will recommend hospitalization if this continues. Insist on weight gain or stop counseling until physical health improves. We will continue to work on accessing parts that control her life and help her grow in being co-consciousness."

I continued to pick wrong relationships repeatedly, looking for love in what seemed like every wrong place that was possible. On one relationship, I thought this young man really cared to the point of having him meet Mary Lu, my mom, and sister and her three kids. I thought this person was it. However, think again as they would say. I got my heart broke again. Picking relationships was as bad as the friends I had chosen. They appeared good on the outside but

looking deep in the inside they were the same. They
were users of drugs, as well as alcohol and me.

I began to get ready to go to West Richland to
talk to the rest of my family about Multiple Personality
Disorder. This was going to be rough because everything
that was in my child hood will be there waiting for me.
Not only the bad stuff but also there will be good
memories as well that will trigger some of the little
alters. One of the most wonderful memories that I will
always hold close to me was at my Uncle Howard's
house. He had a farm full of all kinds of different
animals that my cousin Allan and I would always play
with. He was one of my dearest cousins. The other was
Mae. She was always there for me as I grew up. We
would spend hours in her pool and playing with her
friends in her neighborhood. She was the one that the
alter named Clown would make laugh. I loved to hear
her laugh. She made me feel safe and I loved being with
her. When she was around, Grandpa Jones could not get
me to play his games. She saved me in so many ways.

Allan and I would play with all the creatures that roamed around Uncle Howard's and Aunt Sue's house. I was one girl he could not make squeal over a mouse, snake, or spiders. You see, we both loved all these things even Uncle Howard's tame skunks. We also use to play with their house broke pig named George. Allan and I would go up onto the dyke and throw rocks into the Yakima River. We would walk for miles up there and just played the day away. He was one of my best friends as children growing up. He was such a funny kid. He loved to make other people laugh too.

When we first met, I was six years old and Allan was three years old. Mae and I were with him at Uncle Howard's house and Allan decided to try to play tricks on us "girls." Little did he know I was as strong minded as any boy around. I was a country girl. He proceeded to take out one of the snakes that were in one of the pens and shook it at Mae. Boy did she scream so loudly. I on the other hand found the snake to be so interesting and asked if I could hold it. Allan's mouth dropped wide open in surprise. From this day forward, we were unseparable whenever I went to my Uncle Howard's house.

"I am Chameleon. I know I talk funny because of my accent. I was afraid you would laugh at me. This is the first time I have been out with you. I came around when Lynn was seven years old. Lynn was on a family camping trip. We were in Grandpa Jones van and my cousin Mae was with me. Grandpa called me down from the top bed area to where he was and he began to do things to me. He began to play his games with me that only adults should play when they are married. I cannot go into detail because it was so disgusting. That is when Lynn mentally went to Australia and other different parts of the world and I had to come back here for her. She would pretend to not be around and mentally pretend she was far away from him. One of Lynn's boyfriends hurt her real bad and I had to come out to help her."

Mary Lu helped Chameleon go into what we called the healing light with The Peace Maker but she could not look at the light. Eventually she saw something like beauty and good but she could not understand it. It was the first time any of the alters had seen anything else but black.

Chameleon continues talking to Mary Lu. "We

are going to Richland tomorrow. This trip is for Pal. The trip we took to Grandpa Don's grave was for Sewry. Pal is scared. I want her to go to that trailer and kick the hell out of it. I told Lynn's mom that we will not use nice words and her mom said it was ok for this time only and that we do not use those words at home, we do not talk that way. Lynn's mom is sick and will not be able to go with us. My whole family knows know about what Grandpa Jones did to us. They also know that I am a multiple too. Somebody inside blabbed. Canopy's new boyfriend knows, and learned how to help get Lynn back when one of us is out. Lynn's mom found out that to get Lynn back when one of us is out she just tapped one of her knees and then we go back inside and Lynn comes back."

Mary Lu tapped my knee, I came back, and Chameleon went back inside. A chill came over me and I asked, "Where was I? What happened?"

Mary Lu puts in her report. "She was talking in slight English accent as Chameleon, beginning to trust me as more alters come out. With each session, the traumatic memories are being retrieved. Wants to visit places where the abuse took place. She needs to express lots of anger. She seems confident that she can handle memories. She will be going to Richland tomorrow May 5, 1993. Her Aunt Sue will be available and can call Lynn's mom if she is too overwhelmed. She seems to have a good support system in place."

I went to Richland to do some memory healing at the farmhouse, I stayed at my Uncle Howard's and Aunt Sue's house, and I saw pictures of my grandpa for the first time since he died. I had a very hard time keeping control and was switching repeatedly. I saw one of the pictures of him that was taken on his fiftieth wedding anniversary and I ran out the door. I went for a long walk to try to get back into control. There were so many memories around me that I could not control.

My sister Jane went with me when I went to the old farmhouse. We sat on the grass in the front yard and talked for a while then I knew it was time to go into the green house where Blackie was killed. Memories of me as a child came flashing into my mind. Then I saw a machete off to the side. Then I switched to pal. I held the machete, began to cry, and began to hit the wood in the

57

green house slowly.

Then Jane came by my side and said "No! No! Lynn this is the way to do it!"

She gave me a smile and began to hit the wood frames very hard. Then she gave me back the machete. She said, "Now do not break any glass because we do not want the dog to get his feet cut up but let your anger fly."

Therefore, I did, and with the language of a sailor, I called him every filthy name I could think of. Then all at once I remembered where Grandpa's ashes were and that they were still in the closet in his old bedroom. I visualized what I would do with them. I put some of them on dog crap and cat crap and best of all chicken crap. I began to chant "ASHES TO ASHES AND DUST TO DUST YOU CAN NO LONGER HURT US!" Then I quietly went into the house, whatever I saw that was not breakable I tore off the walls and continued to swear as if he could hear me.

Then I saw a picture of him and took it with me to the silver trailer where most of the abuse took place almost every night when I was young for five years. I

looked at his picture into those abusive eyes and I yelled
and cried, "WHY? WHY DID YOU DO THIS TO ME?"
I looked all around me and sat on the bed where I slept
in every night and saw that my horse posters were still
there after all these years. Flash backs of his nightly
storytelling and the beer he gave me and all the candy he
gave me almost every night. After he gave me some beer
he then would give me tick tacks.

I remembered the guilt trips he would give me if
I tried to say no when he would ask me to play his
games. Then Jane and I talked some more up on top of
the roof of the house where we could see Rattle Snake
Mountain and drank some beer together to celebrate Pals
courage to do what she had done on this most important
day. On this day, the healing began. Then my dad drove
up to the house. So that he would not get to upset about
what I did to the green house and to the house, Jane
stopped him. He saw that I was still upset and after I
calmed down a little more and regained control over
myself my dad and I began to talk for a while.

I learned that he left us because of having flash
backs of the Korean War not because I was a bad little

girl as Grandpa had told me. He told me that he did not know at the time that this was his problem he was just afraid that in time he might hurt us and not mean to. Nightmares seem to get in the way at times. Daddy expressed how much he loved me and that it was not because I was some kind of bad girl or that I had done anything wrong.

The other alters seem to know that now. It was on this day that I not only was able to get to know my sister better, but I also found my very close friend. On one occasion when my mom was with me at Richland, we were at my Uncle Howard's house and apparently, a picture of my grandpa triggered Pal to come out during an evening meal. My mom was able to get Pal into the healing area and hear the light say something about being good and beautiful. Pal wanted to stay with the animals and with Shadow in my safe place.

My mom and I decided to do some more healing at the farmhouse, so I went there once again. We entered the house and I became very frightened and went outside for just a little while. Then I tried again. I had very dark eye makeup on and dark color on my cheeks as if I was an Indian going to war. I guess you could say in a way I was. I was at war against good and evil inside my mind. You might guess who was out doing the fighting. Yep! It was Shadow. I went into my Grandmas bedroom and could see peace and joy in this room.

Then I went into my Grandpas bedroom and fear came over me. I remembered that this is where my Grandpa's ashes were kept. Even though the ashes were in the closet it still felt like he himself was there, looking at me as if he was going to say, "After Blackie you are now next."

Shadow set the ashes of Grandpa on the desk and yelled out her anger. She said very loudly," I hate you and everything you stand for. I hate what you did to us and how you robbed us of our innocents." My mom helped Shadow and yelled aloud too.

My cousins, aunts, and uncles were not aware of everything that had happened to me. Mae who was one of my very special cousins did not know how to act around me. I explained to her to be herself since I never am. In addition, because of Shadow, I began to sing, "Me and my shadow" and because of Pal, I began to quote an old time comedian that use to say, "What a pal, what a pal." Then I began to sing saying, "All of me, why not take all of me?" Mae was laughing so hard I thought she was going to mess her pants right there and then.

It helped her feel more at ease with me being who and what I became, a survivor living with Multiple Personality Disorder.

I found that I had a tendency of running relationships off all the time. It is as if parts of me were very pushy or very immature and this is what most men hate. Gee, I wonder why! On another session with Mary Lu, she used her guided imagery and this is what she found and puts in her report.

"Little Anger spoke with me the best way she could. She was left with a babysitter who had five boys, babysat Lynn, and her sister Jane while their mom went to work. Lynn was two years old and could not play with the older kids and so she stayed at the house with the babysitter all day. The babysitter would ridicule her often. She would make horrible faces at Lynn and this is when Little Anger was created. Eventually Lynn's older sister told their mom and their mom quite working for Lynn's sake and went on welfare. With guided imagery, she was able to experience the rage, hurt, and sadness. The guided imagery was successful today. Lynn has resistance to letting emotions show may be an expression of her desire to stay in control. We will see if cutting up wrists will stop."

Mary Lu helped me find a productive way to put the alter named "The Executioner" to work. Instead of killing the body, I will have him help me with the bad resolved memories by renaming him "The Undertaker" and put him at the gravesite in my safe place. When a memory is resolved, he will bury them in my gravesite up on top of the cliff. We had discovered that this was the alter that caused me to end up in the hospital. Therefore, instead of being destructive we will have him be more constructive. Everyone has a job to do to help keep the core personality safe. Because without "Lynn" the alters would no longer exist.

Another relationship came and gone and I continued seeing Mary Lu every week whether I felt I needed to or not. The hatred of being alone drove me to very unhealthy relationships. I went back to Richland by myself once again and had another memory about my Grandpa Jones. Pal came out and remembered the times Grandpa Jones would wake her up by tickling her feet, legs, and genital area. Then I switched to Angie who does not eat so that I would feel the pain in my stomach and not in my heart. Mary Lu stated that it is time that I start feeling the pain and to stop running away from the memories. Angie told Mary Lu that she was different from Annie who thought she was fat. That Angie is the one who starved to keep her mind off the emotional pain.

This is what Mary Lu puts in her report: "Obvious switching. Lynn's eyes look glazed over. She looks away, talks in a slightly different voice. When her mom came into join us at the end of session Lynn burst into tears for the first time. Lynn remembered that I said it was time to feel the pain in her heart. Her system is working hard to heal. She had nice progress this week."

"Annie has been out" stated Lynn," and we are down 107 lbs and I love it. I am trying not to feel anything and this keeps my mind off my latest boyfriend and everything else. Because I had hurt my knee from a bad fall snow skiing, I might have to have surgery and that means needles."

This is what Mary Lu found during this visit. "I accessed an alter name Little Fear." Little Fear started to cry and asked, "Why are they putting all those needles into me? Mommy was not doing anything to stop them." We also discovered that at times Little Fear is also with another little alter named Baby.

Mary Lu continues writing in her report saying, "I asked for an alter named Courage to come out. Lynn's voice changed and became very strong. Held the hand of the little one and practiced relaxing while a needle went into her arm. Courage said he was willing to help Little Fear and continue to take her hand. She is allowing me to talk to her parts more. Lynn seems less fearful of them. She is surprised to find out that there are two more alters. I will continue to access alters and work on allowing them to let Lynn feel now. She is very fearful of this but it is time. Lynn remains co-conscious. She will plan a visit to her church members soon to discuss a plan for her support and possible re-entry into the congregation."

Mary Lu continues to use guided imagery and it was working really well. My system began to cooperate. I started to allow myself to feel the emotional pain that I hide deep inside for so many years.

The one I call Courage would come out and said to Mary Lu in a deep voice, "I will help her face her pain in her heart. I will also help Baby and Little Fear and will also help seven year old Cheryl."

During one evening when my mom and I were in our apartment, I switched and began to rock on the couch while laying down on it. My mom noticed what was going on and sat by my side. My hands were curled up against my chest and I was fidgeting with my fingers.

My mom gently asked, "Who am I talking to?"

A small child like voice says, "I am Pal."

My mom says hi to Pal and asked her if there was something on her mind that she wanted to talked to her about. Pal says, "Yes, there is a question I wanted to ask you." My mom tells Pal to go ahead and ask her question.

Then Pal asks Mom "what do I call you?"

If only you can imagine what went through my

mom's mind at this time. Here is her twenty six year old daughter asking her what she should call her.

My mom gently says to Pal, "What would you like to call me?"

Pal says in reply, "I don't know! Lynn calls you Mom because you are her mom and to call you Ann would be very rude, so I don't know!"

My mom asks, "Where is Lynn now?"

Pal says, "She went inside and that is when I came out to talk to you." My mom thanks Pal for coming out to talk to her.

My mom tells Pal, "Think about what you want to call me and then let me know." Pal says, "Lynn gets scared and runs inside then we have to come out to help keep the body going. I am so tired now. I think I'll go back inside to the weeping willow tree."

My mom says, "Thank you Pal for coming out to talk to me."

A chill came over me, I blinked and saw my mom looking over me, and she smiled and said, "Welcome back!"

I asked, "What had happened?"

My mom says, "I had a visitor just now."

I asked," Who was out?"

She told me that it was Pal and shared with me their conversation. I looked at my poor mom and all I could say was "YOU ARE KIDDING!"

She smiled and said, "No I am not and I had a wonderful visit and I love Pal as much as I love you."

As spoken about earlier in my story, I had a knee injury when I went skiing with some friends and now we do know that surgery is going to have to happen after all. I have little alters that are very scared of needles and we had to figure out how to help them through the operation with the needles being involved. Mary Lu discovered also that there are about six different alters that smoke. I never smoked before my Grandpa Jones died. I suspect this is a way of self-medicating as memories come up to the surface. The cigarettes made me feel calm and numb. I even did the unthinkable soon after he died which was becoming immoral. I was a virgin till I was 26 years old. I hung around bad people which led to me getting rapped. After that I completely lost it and was on a self-destruction path. Anyway, Mary Lu, my mom, and I came up with a plan on how Courage can hold the hands of the scared ones during surgery, especially during the injections of the needles.

Mary Lu reports, "Lynn was shaking at first, then calm and in control at the end. Pending surgery on her knee is paramount at this time. We did not attempt to do memory work today. She needs to feel safe as possible for now."

On another occasion with Mary Lu, this is what I said, "I just threw up before I came to see you. Annie is out. I remembered my Grandpa Jim who is my mom's stepfather visiting us and saying "HOW DO!" This triggered a memory with my Grandpa Jones. I remembered when he would always say, "HOW DO, YOU DO?" Then he called me into his lap and began to fondle me. Then he took me into the bathroom."

This is what Mary Lu observed during this session: "She is crying very hard and is in a fetal position and rocking. A second time of abreaction she is saying, "I do great!" I will hit Grandpa and walk out."

Then on a third time of abreaction the young alter says, "You will not touch me!" Annie said during the abreaction that if I did not eat I might disappear and he could not touch me anymore."

Mary Lu says, "There is a lot of weeping today. Then she is quite after Annie abreacted and took a doll in her arms to hug. She kept rocking for a few more minutes. The incident triggered the memory. The wand helped her process it. We will see if she is able to eat now. She likes her Grandpa Jim and is able to talk to him a little now for the first time. She says he is safe and is willing to be supportive."

"Well, I went swimming out into the river and cut my knee up on the rocks. Baby is so afraid of needles. We do not want stitches. In addition, I hurt my foot and elbow too. Once again, I am hanging out with the wrong people. If it were not for a stranger who pulled me out of the river, I would have drowned. I never seem to learn my lesson on the people I hung out with. No one cared accept when they needed to use me for something. No, it was not a friend that saved me that day, it was a stranger." The injury to my left knee postponed the surgery.

"Annie was good this week. We ate for three

days then I got on the scale and asked, "How much did I gain?" Instead of asking, "How much did I lose?" I am 110 lbs now. My tummy feels poochy but not bad. I just have not felt like eating the last three days. I got somewhat nauseous when I saw my knee. Some fatty tissue is poking out."

"Shadow has been out. She is mad! I think I am out growing the bar scene. The people there remind me of the kids in school. I never was part of anything."

This was Mary Lu's suggestion regarding this session: "I asked Shadow to rewrite the grade school story. Imagine a party with all of her friends. Then offer someone a coke or snack. Then she would be invited to join their conversation and maybe will be asked to dance. I suggested that all the alters and their friends go skating next week."

When all the alters inside heard this conversation, they liked Mary Lu's ideas and agreed. However, there were times when I did go out to dances with church friends and no one notice I was even around. No boy would ask me to dance or even talk to me. All I found myself doing was sitting in a corner all by myself.

The alters felt like a no body more times than not. This is why some of them are so bitter.

Looking back now, I wonder if the kids at my church saw me switching and they did not feel comfortable around me for reasons they did not know. I am sure that while growing up I did act strange at times and I did not know what I was doing or how I was acting. Other people can sense these things and this can cause people to be uncomfortable around the individual. I am just making a guess here but thinking about it after knowing this about myself it makes me wonder if this was the case when I was growing up.

One other visit to Mary Lu we discussed talking about feelings rather than switching. I was aware of the switching but I stayed co-conscious. I told Mary Lu that Annie was still under the weeping willow tree and was doing well. I had not yet buried the memory of what Annie went through but Undertaker waits at the gravesite for when Annie is finally ready to let the memories go.

This is what Mary Lu puts in her report: "She has dark circles under her eyes. She showed me her knee. There is about ¼ of an inch gash on her left knee. I see some serum oozing, but it is not infected. Her legs are extremely thin. She is talking in monotone (probably Shadow). Session last week was very intense. She wants to back off and focus on present for today."

There have been times during my treatment that I found myself in some very uncomfortable situations. One of the adult alters would want to date and be intimate with a boyfriend and a younger alter would feel that she was being raped. The man would not have any clue that he was sleeping with a different person than he began the night with, to him it was his girlfriend and to someone like Annie, well she would feel like she was being violated.

In Mary Lu's report, she puts this, "One piece missing here about how she feels compelled to go to bars with her friends. The cycle continues to repeat with Annie feeling she was being raped. Annie has unfinished memory of her Grandpa Jones. She has deep desire to go back to worshipping God. She will be having knee surgery very soon and the little alters are very scared. I will make home visit if she is unable to come to the clinic. We will continue to work on her Grandpa Jones memories and how she gets seduces into relationships easily."

My knee surgery came and went and Mary Lu did what she promised. She did home visits with me until my leg got stronger. We worked very hard in helping Annie to not so easily be pressured into relationships against her will. Annie gets very lonely and finds herself in compromising situations. She gets frightened because she remembers how Grandpa Jones made her feel that if she did not do what he asked of her he would hurt her more. Therefore, this has been the case with these men that she finds in the bars.

Mary Lu says this, "Lynn has increased awareness of her internal process that leads to her being victimized so often."

As time passed on I became stronger and I grieved and relived the memories all over again. Something began to happen and it was a very strange feeling. It was time that two of the alters began to integrate. They wanted to do this at home but wanted to be with Mary Lu for the first integration. I also asked that my mom be a part of this as well.

Little Cheryl who is four years old came out and this is what she said, "I want to thank you Mamma for hugging my tears away. I also want to thank you Mary Lu for all your help. It is time for me to grow up now with big Cheryl who is seven years old."

With guided imagery little Cheryl and big Cheryl went into the river in my safe place. As the water ran over them, they began to feel bigger. I felt a head ache coming on then some resistance then in a few minutes I felt calmer. I began to have memories of being twelve years old and playing with my German Sheppard that had passed away. In addition, I began to remember playing with my Grandpa Don. The Executioner was standing by the gravesite waiting to bury the resolved memories that these two little alters were done with. Little Cheryl cringe very hard as she was saying good-bye to Mamma. Nevertheless, little did we know their work was not done yet? There was more to their stories than they knew.

DADDY

My daddy's a cowboy; he is always on the go.
Every time I would see him I would always feel a glow.

I would look out my window and wonder where
he would be I then realized I never knew my daddy.

Now my daddy and I have many places and
things to see, I would wonder, will I ever again see my
daddy?

Remembering the times he would walk through
the door, I would cry, Daddy, Daddy, your back to stay!
The next thing I knew he was driving away.

My mama would come and hug my tears away,
she'd simply say, "He'll be back again someday."

Even though that was many years ago and I am
now a young lady, I know I will forever be my daddy's
baby.

This is what Mary Lu put in her report,

"Animated at first, then weeping as little Cheryl thanked

Mamma for hugging her tears away. Then she begins to

be more serious as more memories started. Lynn says

that there were actually twenty-four alters; there was a

pretender, Now she has twenty-two with today's merger,

so we thought. The process of healing is going very well.

76

The first merger heralds the beginning of fusion."

The Pretender is an alter who pretends she is fine and doing well but in reality she is not doing very well at all but does not want anyone to know this. She is afraid of people but pretends she is not because it causes these people to know her or the fear she has inside. She pretends to be happy or pretends that everything inside is just fine especially towards her family.

So far, these are our findings since the beginning of my therapy. First, there is Lynn, the core personality. Then there is Sewry who is thirteen years old and loves her Grandpa Don very much. Then there is The Peace Maker who brings peace and light to everyone who is inside my safe place. There is Little Cheryl who is four years old and Big Cheryl who is seven years old.

They were created when my dad left me when I was four and when my mom and dad got a divorce when I was seven years old.

There is Pal who is eight years old. She was created when my Grandpa Jones killed my pet rooster Blackie. There is also Chameleon who talks as if she is from Australia or England. There is also Annie who thinks she is fat. In addition, there is Angie who starves the body as a way to punish herself with pain because she feels that she is bad. There is also the one called The Clown who loves to make other people laugh because; it helps her to not think about the pain that she feels.

There is Little Anger who is two years old. She came about when a baby sitter made fun of her and scared her real bad. One called The Quiet One is ten years old. She came out when I had to move to Portland and be apart from all my family in West Richland. There is also Little Fear who is afraid of needles. This fear was the result of when I was dying as a baby and penicillin shots saved my life.

Then there is the twelve year old who still plays with my German Shepard who died. Of course, we must never forget Shadow. She does not trust anyone and is quite still when it comes to being around people. Then there is one called the Executioner who we renamed as the Undertaker so that he does not hurt the body anymore but helps bury the memories when they are resolved. We also have Canopy who seeks for someone to love her and can never find it. There is an alter that I cannot seem to find a name for. No Name. She wonders around being very busy doing anything she can do to not think about what is hurting inside. Maybe if I thought about it hard enough I might have called her the wonderer. She cannot seem to sit still for very long in one place.

There is also an alter named Bitter. She is very harsh and sarcastic. Then there is one called Big Anger who is verbally violent and yells a lot when he gets upset. In addition, there is an alter named Courage. He is not afraid of anyone and helps the others feel safe when everyone gets scared for some reason such as a memory. We also have one called Baby who is very afraid of needles just like Litter Fear. Then as we just discovered, there is The Pretender, who is afraid of people and their anger but pretends she is not. There was also the Denier who refuses any of this to be true and claims that this has all been made up and is in our heads. Well guess what? This condition is made up and it is all in my head. I created the system to survive the torture and fear that was brought onto me as a child. This was my way of "going away" from all of the badness. I created these alters for myself, they saved my life. These alters I made up in my head saved me from going crazy and from dying. Hence, this is why Mary Lu called this a "gift." Well there we have it. The list just gets larger and larger.

"I feel inside that we are almost finished. I am working on my journal and so is my mom. I want you to add something to my journal so people will know the truth."

I kept talking to Mary Lu saying, "It is important that we believe even though this was not a satanic cult abuse. I am a multiple and people need to believe us."

I realized at this moment what I just said. I came to reality and finally admitted what this is that I have been living with in my mind my whole life. Like with any addiction or disorder the first step to recovery is admitting you have a problem and facing it and accepting it.

I continued talking to Mary Lu saying, "Shadow has been out a lot. I had a rough week. The two who integrated last week are only partly together. I can see them and they are no problem but it feels weird."

Pal came out to finish her story about grandpa killing Blackie and this is how we did it. Mary Lu used guided imagery and had Pal go to the stream and have The Peace Maker help her wash off the blood and put a rock on Blackies grave. Pal began to say goodbye to Blackie and to the good times she did have with Grandpa Jones and the times she remembers riding on the hood of the lawn mower. In addition, I had to say goodbye to the memories of going to the spud nut shop, where he use to take her all the time.

Mary Lu puts this in her report, "System continues to heal itself. The memories are finalizing and being resolved. Lynn still appears to be very thin and is probably still anorexic. There may be more work there to be resolved."

Pal came out one day while my mom and I went to a religious meeting. Pal ran to the back room and my mom followed and sat by Pal. A man came in and smiled gently at Pal and Pal asked my mom, "He does not know does he?"

My mom gently told Pal, he does not know you Pal but he knows Lynn."

The next visit I had with Mary Lu, Annie was out. I could not eat in fact I was afraid of food all together. I was out of control and she came out to keep me preoccupied with food and weight. I kept looking away as I spoke with Mary Lu. I could not keep eye contact with her or anyone else no matter how hard I tried. As time went by, I became more aware of the switching, but I could not control it quite yet.

I became involved with a man that was in prison, he seemed very good, and we became friends then fell in love, so I thought. He wanted to marry me and so we got married. After a short time, I realized that Lynn was not the one who got married. It was an alter named Canopy who had married him. It hurt many people and it worried my mom and sister very much. After some time I got stronger and got an annulment. I have a very confusing, and complicated gift because it seemed to other people that I always knew what I was doing and knew of the decisions I was making, but in reality, I did not. So I guess you could say that at times this condition is not always considered a gift regarding the poor choices the alters make and get me into trouble. This caused a lot of confusion and pain to those that were involved. Like I said to my mom many times, "I do not know why I do the things I do. I do not want to do these bad things but I cannot seem to stop it,"

"I feel strange. Something is unfinished. The two Cheryl's have not completely merged yet. This is the date I went into the psychiatric ward last year." (October 27, 1992)

At the end of the session, Mary Lu writes this, "Ending session with Lynn remembering when she was eighteen years old and tried to die because of feelings of being lonely and in despair. I am unable to get to cognition. She is feeling a bit fragmented."

Mary Lu continues saying, "She is teary at times and keeps looking away. There are still some unfinished memories. She is not ready for full integration yet. We need to see what else this week will bring up. Next week we will work on talking about feelings rather than acting them out or going into anorexia in order not to feel."

I went to a religious meeting and I saw one of the elders there. Chameleon came out and I went to the bathroom for about forty-five minutes. I felt so alone

beings no one could talk to me because I was dis-
fellowshipped. Annie had been out for a while and I lost
five pounds.

Annie came out during one of my sessions with
Mary Lu and this is what she had to say. "Yes I want to
go to the hospital. At least someone there would care.
The people are nice, they talk to me, and they give a
damn. No one at the place we went to for that religious
meeting cares. I know that God cares but no one else
does."

Mary Lu puts this in her report. "I sent Annie to
the healing light to ask for the truth. She saw herself
kneeling and pleading for help." Mary Lu continues to
write. "Lynn struggles to stay an adult. Her only support
is her mom at this point. She is tearful and weeping as
Annie. She is also angry and has her hands in a fist as
Shadow when she came in. There is much switching
today. Her emotions are out of control somewhat. She
has begun to admit that she needs more help than she
had thought. Lynn wants Annie to go to Anorexia
meeting with me on Saturday. I'll continue to support
her process and efforts to get help for Annie, the

anorexic part."

Throughout these years of therapy, I went into a financial tailspin. I spent money faster than I made it. I spent most of my time going to bars to drink the voices in my head away. It was a mixed up time for me. I did not know whether I was coming or going. I guess you could say I was going, going, gone;

I went to the anorexia workshop. It was wonderful but also upsetting. I heard the speaker ask, "What do you not want to face?" It was anger for one thing. I was angry with my dad for abandoning me, never paying for child support, never being around when I needed him. I was angry with the elders in my congregation for not trying to understand me and in what I am going through. I felt like no one gave a damn around me except for my mom and sister. I was just angry! Annie wanted to weigh 105 lbs. I think this was fear of food and the fear of being fat was a fear of feelings. I did not want to feel at all, but I had to feel even though I did not want to.

I recall on one other session Mary Lu met an alter she hardly ever saw. This is what she says in her report.

"Lynn switched to a new part I do not believe I hardly ever saw. She identified herself as the Indian part and began to speak in Native American. She said her name was Klatawa Talapus that means Running Coyote. However, she hated this name because Grandpa Jones gave her this name. She is The Peace Maker because she brings peace and harmony to everyone inside. Every night she says "Mamook Hiu WaWa Kopa Sagla Tyee." This means, "Speak a lot with God." She wants her new name to be "The Peace Maker." The Peace Maker has been available to help the little ones but never spoke to Mary Lu until now. We knew she was there but this is the first time she has told us why she exists.

Pal had a lot of anger and she has every right to be angry. The Peace Maker took Pal by the hand and took her to the healing light. She told Pal about an Eagle who represents power, peace, and wisdom. She also told Pal to go with the Eagle. In addition, that she will teach her justice and love. In addition, to know the truth and the truth will set her free. The Peace Maker is very religious and believes in the almighty God who created all things and because of him all things exists. The Peace

Maker has coal black hair that hangs past her waist. She has dark brown eyes and dark skin. She is tall, slender, and beautiful. Mary Lu saw during this session that I was nicely groomed and my makeup was on impeccable. I had a soft smile about me and I was alert most of the time. She noticed that I was somber and kind that is the way The Peace Maker is.

Mary Lu says this about the Peace Maker, "Is this a new Part? On the other hand, is this one the one that has been watching? Is this part ready to integrate or not? We will have to wait and see."

"I am losing weight again. Annie was out." Mary Lu asked Annie to go to the light. However, she refused; Annie said if she did, she would cry. She wants to be in control. Mary Lu tried gently prodding her again to go to the light. Annie was very defiant, and refused. Then all at once a surge of anger came over me and I switched to another alter whom Mary Lu had never met.

This is what Mary Lu saw, "Screaming and pounding on her legs, saying, "I hate him, I hate him."

Mary Lu asked who was out and the strong angry voice says, "I am Violet which stands for physical violence when I get mad."

Mary Lu asked her not to hurt the body or Lynn but hit the chair instead. Violet tells Mary Lu that she has to inflect pain because we are all bad. After three minutes of this, I switched again and began to weep. At this time, all I wanted now was to be held and rocked. Mary Lu called my mom in. As one time before, just after I got dis-fellowshipped I crawled onto my mom's lap and she began to rock me as if I was a very young child again. The first time I did this to my mom, she knew something was very wrong. Well you can only imagine what went through my mom's head. I had dark circles under my eyes and I was wearing sweats and hitting myself repeatedly. I was so afraid to feel because I never did feel until now.

The elders in the congregation I use to attend could not understand that my conduct was out of my control and it made me angry. Pal was out a lot of the time and so was Canopy.

Mary Lu suggested, "Take Pal to the healing light and ask for the truth."

There was a lot of resistance. Pal states that she is

afraid to feel the pain. During this visual imagery, The Peace Maker came out. She prayed for the Eagle to come and help Pal. The Peace Maker states that Pal was too little to be with the elders and that she had lied to them when they asked if she felt bad. She really did feel bad but was so confused that she agreed to whatever they said.

Mary Lu puts this in her report. "There is obvious switching from Anger to sad, to Pal then to Lynn. Her mood is changing rapidly. She is at her calmest when she is The Peace Maker."

Mary Lu continues writing in her report, "The meeting with the elder's at one time triggered guilt and shame that was inflicted by my Grandpa Jones." She continues, "Parts resistant to the healing light. They might need some gentle prodding to be able to face and accept the truth."

It was very difficult to continue in getting stronger because some of the alters were afraid that if they did they would lose Mary Lu because I would not be able to see her any more if I intergraded. In addition, I was afraid that if I was not a multiple any more my mom would not be able to speak to me any more either because I was dis-fellowshipped.

Mary Lu says in her report. "There is resistance in merging together for fear of losing me if she does. Her own healing process is continuing to happen anyway."

One morning I had a dream. It was as if a fog was rolling in and all the parts were coming together. On one occasion, Pal asked my mom, "How come Grandpa abused me when I was little?" As if, she was growing up. The dream was as if they were all merging together. Not just merging two by two but all together. It was the strangest feeling I had ever encountered. Mary Lu reports. "Her mom continues to support her process and for her to get ready for integration. Lynn will probably need several months of post-integration help. She is actually doing well."

SHADOW

I see a shadow that roams within, she is bold
and strong, she will not let anyone in.

She lives in a world, which is dark, and cold,
her story is mysterious, what will it unfold?

When it comes to people she lacks trust, for
they have hurt her with a mighty thrust.

The pain she feels, she refuses to reveal for
the less people know the less they
can hurt and steal.

A woman of beauty is what I see, as she takes
off her hood and shows her identity.

She speaks to no one unless the need arise,
she is my power, my might, she fills my soul
with pride.

Her eyes are black, her hair long dark brown,
and the shape of her smile is a stern glaring
frown.

A woman of beauty is what I see; she hides
deep inside of me. She is my   backbone of
strength, and she gives me security.
She speaks to no one unless the need may be.

Her story is mysterious she refuses to tell. To
find the truth the pain will be hell."

April 15, 1994

"Pal was out the other day. She seems to be older. I guess she is almost done with the memories in Richland. I might have to go back in the springtime to tie up some loose ends. I might walk through the green house one more time and check out the trailer once more. My Grandma has a picture of me holding Blackie, my pet rooster and I want that. Pal still does not know that Grandpa has died. This is all so weird!" I feel a sharp pain in my chest and my hands are tingling. I am switching again! I do not know who it is yet. Oh my god! Can there be twins? It is Shadow and she has taken off her black hood. She looks just like The Peace Maker! They are twins! They look the same." I had with me a picture of an Indian maiden with long black hair and big dark brown eyes and showed it to Mary Lu. "This is what shadow and The Peace Maker looks like." Shadow is the dark side of me and The Peace Maker is the peaceful and religious part of me.

On a separate session with Mary Lu, I stated, "I do not want to be here because I know something awful will happen." I told Mary Lu, "I am angry, bitter, I have

92

chest pains, my speech is slurred, and I have blurry vision. I am a mess! Last night Anger and Bitter were out." Mary Lu asks me to check inside my mind. Therefore, I did, and this is what I saw. I saw Pal and Sewry by the ocean. Anger was on top of the mountain. Angie and Annie were under the cliff, Shadow had her hood back on. The little ones were under the weeping willow tree. The Peace Maker was in the healing light. The scene was clearer this time and it was not as hazy as before. I continued to tell Mary Lu, "Something is wrong. We are not happy. I feel much fear." I also saw that Violet was dressed in black. Remembering again of the time when my mom and I were reading the magazine article about incest when I was fourteen years old.

The thought about Grandpa lying to us made us madder and it was time to heal from it. The fact that my mom believed me was a big relief and I felt safe to express this anger. "We hate being lied to." Shadow said to Mary Lu. Shadow continues to speak, "He lied to us about this being our fault. He should pay for his lies. As the session moved on I began to recall Grandpa's death.

How I was afraid to let anyone else in my family know that I cried over his death. What he did was terrible and a few people in my family hated him for what he did. As Mary Lu and I kept talking, I realized that on some level I still loved the good part of him, which was the storyteller, and the Grandpa that took me to the spud nut shop. We did have a few good memories. However, the bad ones over took the good memories of him. The good memories I can remember was going bug hunting with my duck Happy, and when I would crow like my rooster Silky. Grandpa never knew if it was I, or the young rooster crowing because we were both bad at it. This is what Mary Lu puts in her report, "Pal appears very tired and hostile at first. She wept as she recalled Grandpa's death. She seemed to be smiling and appears to be peaceful at the end."

There were times when I switched a lot and never knew who I was from one day to the next. I remember one time when Shadow spoke with Mary Lu saying, "I am so tired of doing Lynn's dirty work all the time. I wish she would set her own boundaries." I checked inside and saw what appeared to be Pal getting bigger and how she felt so upset because no one noticed. When I told my mom, she got Pal a gift. It was a silver little image of a child curled up in a ball called, "The child within." I got a rope silver chain to wear with it and to this day, I still wear it. I was struggling about going to a religious meeting because I remembered how my Grandpa used to say that his games were ok with God. I also had trouble in getting Annie to tell her story because when she is out, she is becomes afraid of food and gaining weight.

On one occasion, I went to cannon Beach with a girlfriend. As soon as I saw Hay Stack Rock, I began to cry. My friend understood, I explained to her what I was feeling and when I switched to Sewry. I looked out into the ocean and visualized a ship passing by out in the far distance and said, "I do not want to let go but now is the time." In my mind's eye, I heard Grandpa Don's ship honking telling Sewry that he loved her and that he will see her again someday. Sewry gently replied back saying, "I love you Grandpa. Thank you for everything you gave me. You did more for me in four years that I knew you than my other Grandpa did for me in my whole life."

Fourteen years of grieving and in all this time Sewry sat under the weeping willow tree. She wrote a letter to Grandpa Don, She put in a bottle, corked it and threw it into the ocean towards the ship. As he sailed away, he honked the ships horn for the last time. Keep in mind that this all was happening in my mind's eye. This was the hardest cry I had done in a very long time. My friend that was with me cried too. I prayed to my heavenly father to give me the courage to integrate and to give me wisdom. I prayed for the courage to find my way back into serving him once again. The ship is gone and the bottle followed. It is over. Sewry can now integrate. I felt beauty, joy, and freedom for the first time.

In my session with Mary Lu, I saw that The Undertaker began to dig a hole to be ready to bury Sewry's memories. Through guided imagery, I experienced my first integration. It went like this, Sewry wanted to be in the ocean in my safe place in my mind's eye. I went with her near the shore where we could touch the ground. We began to swim in the ocean then Sewry gave me a very big hug. There was a little bite of resistance and a few shivers came over me then Sewry went inside the core personality's body, which was I.

I was uncomfortable at first because of headaches and a crawly feeling came over me. It felt and looked as if we were like shells of hollow dolls, one inside the other. The inner one hallow so that there is room for the others. I was tearful at first then I appeared bright and happy. I was visibly shaking as I intergraded with Sewry the thirteen year old alter. I felt so tired at the end of all this. I looked at my mom and smiled saying, "It is finally happening and it is just the beginning."

Mary Lu adds this into her report, "System continuing to heal. The Undertaker is now digging a hole to bury the resolved memories of Grandpa Don. The integration is beginning as she works through final memories and the final goodbyes. May still have borderline traits but will work on those as need arises. "I am so angry! This week I woke up during the night and was hitting myself. Violet was out. I went out with two couples and I felt like a freak. I do not fit in anywhere. I hate it! I am such a mess."

Mary Lu says this in her report, "Eyes wide opened, jaws clenched, fists clenched, some tears, she is mostly raging." Mary Lu continues to write, "Discussed healing process. The rage is a normal part of it. Being with married couples is painful right now and will continue to be until she is able to accept herself. Discussed going to a religious meeting with her mom. Decided on staying there a half hour and then leave whether she likes it or not. That will get her out of the all or nothing mode. Her rage is understandable. There is still much healing to be resolved to be able to get the rage out rather than turning inward. In addition, she needs to accept the pain of loneliness in ways that are more appropriate. We will work on taking care of her in social situations. We will attempt to address Violet and

Annie, the two most destructive parts and the ones who seem to try to divert her attention from the pain she feels."

The days would come and go and I would still go to the bars but I noticed something different this time. I was getting stronger and stronger. I could resist the temptations of over drinking or men flirting with me. I was learning what it was like to be in a constructive type control, instead of the destructive type control. What do you know? I was finally growing up inside and it felt so good. I would go to the religious meetings with my mom and make a deal with Pal that we would only stay for a half hour at a time then we would leave and it worked out. I knew I still had a lot of work cut out for me to do yet but I also knew that I had come a very long way too.

Mary Lu puts this in her next report, "Animated and nicely groomed today with jeans and a black leather jacket with the necklace that had her newly acquired child within charm that her mom gave her that represents Pal. There was no apparent switching today. The integration is holding and she is able to tolerate a little of the religious meetings now. She is showing good assertiveness at bars. Her ego strength is building nicely."

Pal

"Well you are going to get your money's worth today. Look at me! My hands are trembling and my speech is all mixed up. Something has come up. We went to a religious meeting last night and I heard them say, "How children can disgrace their parents." I think it is Pal. She is terrified! Something is happening. The rug is moving. The bookcase is moving. I have a real bad headache." Pal came out trembling. "He is going to get me! NO, NO, STOP! Pal continues to describe some awful conduct that Grandpa Jones is doing with a collie dog she had on the farm in the garage that burnt down. Then he apparently does something bad to Pal. He took Blackie and me to the green house. He broke Blackies wings. Soon, he broke Blackies legs. I had to hear my pet scream in pain. Then he broke his neck and then there was total silence. He tells Pal or at the time he thought was I, that if I tell anyone he would have something bad happen to me just like he did to my pet chicken. I once again during visual imagery see Grandpa breaking Blackies wings and legs, and then killing him.

It was on this day Pal was created and I ran away mentally.

Pal continues to tell Mary Lu, "Now that I have told someone, he is going to hurt me too because Grandpa said so." Mary Lu called The Peace Maker to take Pal to the healing light to release her pain. In guided imagery, The Peace Maker put her hands up high and the pain went to the light. The light was warm as if God Almighty were saying that he would be the one to judge Grandpa. In my mind, I heard something say, "She has a much better chance of everlasting life than Grandpa does." However, that was completely up to God not anyone else. The healing light helped me feel that Lynn was good and beautiful in Gods eyes. The Peace Maker says, "We have to face the memory of why Lynn throws up and cannot eat."

My mom was asked to come into the room at the end of the session and she saw me sitting in the corner of the room trembling and weeping and screaming for Grandpa to not hurt me. My mom knelt down and began to rock me as she always did. At the end of our session, Mary Lu puts this in her report, "Nearing the end of the painful memories. Lynn will need continued support as she intergrades and starts to function as a singleton."

I wrote a lot about my thoughts of death. I felt I had nothing else to look forward to and thought that death was the only way out of this pain I was feeling inside repeatedly. For so many years, I have hidden this pain and now I have to feel this trauma all over again. I had felt that I became to be a real mental mess. My Grandma Jones would visit me and I knew she knew that my Grandpa had abused me and a part of me was ashamed and embarrassed. She had always loved me and was such a good grandma. I have wonderful memories of her as a child and clear through my adult hood. .

I wanted a man to love me so badly that it hurt deep inside. You would think I would feel the opposite after everything I went through. However, I have read that it is not uncommon for an abused girl to look for love anywhere she can because she had never experienced love before from a man while she was young. I guess this describes me.

I looked in every wrong place possible is seemed, and I paid for it too. I felt I had to please the men I met or they would abandon me or hurt me just as if Grandpa did and my dad did by abandoning me. Grandpa said I should please everyone. However, it got me nowhere but heartache every time. Another memory had come to the surface on one occasion with Mary Lu. Pal came out and began to cry very hard. She remembered Grandpa playing a sexual game with me that only married couples should do. Pal felt so ashamed and ugly.

We went to the healing light with The Peace Maker. Pal decided to stay there for the rest of the week. Pal felt that there was more to finish regarding the memories in the green house, the garage that burnt down, and the trailer that we slept in every night. I fear that there might be another part inside. I heard something rambling in my head.

Mary Lu puts this in her report, "Let her go at her

own pace. Will work on whatever she brings up. Will support her strengths and encourage her to welcome any other parts that might still be hiding or stuck." On another occasion with Mary Lu, she checked on Pal by doing guided imagery. This is what she sees, "There is more for Pal to tell about the incident with her grandpa in the trailer. She says she has been telling the least awful stuff and there is more. Pal feels so ashamed but has to tell the rest of her story."

She gives more details about how her grandpa abused her and made her do things to herself while he watched. The details got so painful that I had pal go to the healing light with The Peace Maker. Then the two of them went to the river and got in for a while. (Keep in mind this is in my minds safe place) Pal drank some of the water then went to the weeping willow tree. The Peace Maker went back to the light where she sits quietly. The other alters were quiet on this day. "Annie and shadow still refuse to go to the light. We suspect there is something behind their resistance." Mary Lu continues to report, "Lynn has some new friends but still finds people who like to hang out in taverns." It could be

105

the reason why Annie and Shadow do not go to the healing light. Because they are afraid, it will tell them the truth about how unclean their conduct is and the truth hurts.

"I am so tired." I began to tell May Lu,

"I do not want to be here. Annie is out too. I just want to get this over with for the last time. Shadow is out too. I am depressed, lonely, lost, scared, and confused. So how is that for starters today?"

Annie came out and began to tell Mary Lu her story,

"I joined the system when I was nine years old. Grandpa Jones put me in the bathtub and began to fondle me. I had to sit on his lap and he touched me more. I began to come out often when Lynn was twelve years old but no one knew it was I at the time. Then I came out again when I was twenty-one years old. Lynn does not want to feel the pain so I come out to help Lynn. The kids in school use to call me terrible names all the time.

106

They would call me Niger lips, fish face, fish lips, grease pit, and chink eyes. Every feature of my face was made fun of. I felt like the ugliest person on earth. After being lied to all my life, it was easy to believe everything that these kids called me."

Mary Lu asked me to sit by The Peace Maker near the healing light. Again, the light in my safe place was warm and the light said that I needed inner peace.

I remembered going to school in West Richland, the kids did not want anything to do with me. My best friend would only play with me at home, where no other kids could see her play with me. While on the bus coming and going to school, I would look out the window and dream that I was on a horse running far away from everyone that was mean. I pictured running into the sunset and never coming back. These brief moments were the only time I felt at peace. Some family members, I felt like they did not like me very well because they did not understand me at the time. Mary Lu asked Annie to look into the water to see her reflection beside The Peace Maker. She saw that The Peace Maker was the prettier of the two. Mary Lu encouraged Annie to sit by The Peace Maker this week and then to let her know what happens.

Mary Lu discussed in building an imaginary bomb shelter as a place in which the alters who are the most angry could do whatever they want to Grandpa Jones. She said that we needed to be careful to keep the little ones that still loved him out of the shelter. Mary Lu talked to Annie. Annie was still beside The Peace Maker. She knows that Lynn wants to go back to her religion. Annie wants to keep herself preoccupied so that she does not feel. It will be hell if she does.

The rage inside kept increasing. Mary Lu suggested that Annie must be getting tired of her job and Mary Lu could see she really loved Lynn and was trying to protect her. Mary Lu continues to put in her report, "Ambivalence about handling her loneliness while waiting to be reinstated in her church seems paramount. Has one friend at work but that is only for a few hours on each week. Annie thinks she should stay anorexic to drive the men away so she can get reinstated." Mary Lu suggests that we find a positive addiction for Annie. "We will have Annie do some bible study lessons with The Peace Maker. We will also contact a support group for anorexics. Lynn is angry, defiant, weeping at times. She appears tired and pale. Annie feels trapped. To give up her defenses means to feel and to feel means to hurt and face the rest of the bad memories. To go back to her religion means to give up partying and being at taverns. This is the only place for socialization right now."

Mary Lu spent the first half hour of one session with me and with another person with Multiple Personality Disorder because I have never met one before. This sounds very strange, but I needed to ask some questions and see for myself what others see when I switch or just act like myself if that is at all possible. Then during my visit with Mary Lu's other patient I felt a shift inside me and said, "I have an alter that is denier. I felt this alter that is in denial. I said, "Oh my God! I have a denier part. This alter thinks we are all faking this to get attention and she denies that this can all be real inside my mind." The other patient watches as this is going on, she assures me that it is normal to be in a state of denial.

Mary Lu stated this in her report, "I will attempt to access denier again. We will encourage Annie and Violet to go to the healing internal light. All parts who do not worship God are very resistant to the internal light."

"Annie is out. She is angry."

Mary Lu asked me to encourage Annie to go to the healing light and ask for help inside. There was a lot of resistance. Annie listed her rage by saying, "I feel unwanted, I have no marriage partner, and I feel fat and ugly."

Mary Lu asked Annie to lay all feelings down and ask for the power to control her feelings. Annie could not deal with them now. Mary Lu saw that I was skin and bones and very pale. I finally acknowledged that Annie was not healthy and she needed help. I had left Mary Lu's office very tired and very hungry and had promised her that I would try to eat something. After my visit with the other patient, I realized I am not alone. I was comforted to know that this disorder is very real. I realized that this is not some made up freak show to excuse me to do what is wrong.

I Continued going to different bars and meeting unhealthy people that in time would take advantage of me without me knowing how to stop them. I would dress up with my Indian jewelry, boots, and jeans at one place or I would dress up in a small skirt and high heel shoes at another place. It all depends on who took me out so to speak. Each alter had their own memory box that they would put unresolved bad memories in and Annie decided to leave her box in the healing light by visual imagery. The twelve year old in my mind was playing with her German Sheppard in the yard of my safe place. She did not want to deal with the fact that her only best friend had died of old age. My Sheppard died when she was fifteen years old.

Mary Lu tried to get Annie to have control over spiritual things instead of food. Annie resisted against this very much because to change control over food would be saying she had a problem. We tried to give Annie a new job to do that was constructive instead of destructive. After all, this worked with the Executioner in renaming him the Undertaker. Instead of killing the body, he now helps bury the bad memories as they are finished being dealt with. Maybe if we could help Annie find a more positive way to control her fears then the other alters could feel safer.

Mary Lu attempted to get other parts to talk to each other and to Annie about how they feel about her controlling the food. There was a lot of resistance to this. Annie is aware that she needs to morn over her pet that died. He German Shepard was her friend too. As long as she obsesses on food, she does not think about their Shepard's death. I had a habit of ignoring the hunger pains that in time I hardly felt hungry anymore. Whenever I tried to eat, I felt sick to my stomach or I was full with just two bites.

There were times that I could not face my own

bedroom because of the paintings that hung on my wall that Grandpa Jones had painted. Another item was an old stagecoach with two horses in front of it that he had made. There was also a Siamese cat on top of it. The mess in my room got worse and worse with time. I had realized that I had been running from these things for a very long time and did not know what I was doing until now. I cried at the fact that I could not be proud of the items that he had created with such talent on the account of what he did to me as a little girl. If I did start to cry over him I would make myself stop because I felt it was a sign of weakness and that I was supposed to hate him not miss him. When I say, miss him I mean missing the good memories that I did have with him.

My messy room, we found out was symbolic of how I felt inside. My inside world was full of chaos and confusion. I was finally ready to face my bedroom and try to organize it and clean up the mess just as if I was trying to with the mess in my mind. I needed to put everything in its place and throw away what I felt was not needed anymore. Fix the things that were broken and begin to heal what was damaged just like my inside world that I was living in.

'Mary Lu puts this in her report, "Next week we will continue the grief work. I will consider targeting the alters that feel it is weak to cry. The other parts of her system have no trouble with tears." On one other session Pal was out and spoke to Mary Lu stating, "I am so tired. I have not had much sleep. I have been grumpy all day. I have not touched my bedroom. Just facing that anger is too much. I do not want to live."

I did some hard drugs on the weekend so I did not have to hear the voices anymore, then I got paranoid. It was terrible. I felt like such a disgrace to everyone. I have hurt my friends and my mom. I have let everyone down! I am a failure, a total failure. I know I have to face this anger. I just do not want to be a Jones anymore. I will have any other last name but Jones.

I feel so bad that I treated my other grandpa so badly. I just thought all grandpas were bad. However, my Grandpa Don and Grandpa Jim were just the opposite and I could not say sorry until it was too late.

Mary Lu says this is her report, "Last session very painful. There is much resistance to feeling her feelings. There is much rage, sadness, and grief. All negative feelings shut off as much as she can and yet they are all so close to the surface that she is becoming intimidated. Lynn continues to work at embracing her feelings."

When people have to deal with their own mental issues or health problems, sometimes other family members get lost in the shuffle. I can only speak for myself, but I was so consumed on how I was feeling and what I was going through that I did not take into consideration on what my mom was going through. Here she is living under the same roof as I did and had to watch me be destructive with no regard in what she was going through at the same time. The pain she must have gone through. She is just one of so many loved ones that were left behind along the way to recovery. We become so self- absorbed in our own selves, we forget about the ones that love us so much.

My mom has a story to tell in how she got through the trauma of watching her daughter go through a living hell. Her experience and story is one of many parents out there who do not know what to do in helping the mentally ill. Her technique is a successful one that might help a parent or a sibling that maybe going through this same nightmare. We are all different with different situations. Therefore, what may have worked for one parent may not work for another parent. However, her experience can lay a foundation on how to start the recovery process.

Our journey in recovering from Multiple Personality Disorder has not ended but getting through the pain and helping me become co-conscious is a very big stepping-stone and one that has helped me to be able to live a somewhat healthier life. Like I had mentioned in the beginning, if you get nothing else out of her story, take this much with you. Listen and be available to the best of your ability. Take the time; to not just say what you feel would be the right thing, but to hear with your heart your child's pain. Listening was the most powerful tool my mom used. This is her story.

Multiple Personality Disorder Through A Mother's Eyes

December 1992

It first came into my head to write about this at 6:30am one December morning. It was just a gossamer trace of a thought in the back of my mind. I was asleep, you see, in that unreal transition from sleep to wakefulness. Wakefulness came with a bump when I realized that the child's voice I was hearing was no longer a part of my dream.

"Pain..Pain? See? Pain."

The laugh I heard reminded me of a child's giggle or the 'baby' voice people sometimes use when talking to their pets-especially baby pets. Since we had a brand new kitten at the time it did not seem unusual. Only the words seemed odd. I listened carefully. "See? Pain," I sat up carefully and arranged my face into what I hoped was a careful lack of expression.

"Hello," I said, hoping not to frighten her. "How are you?"

I hoped my face would stay the way I had so carefully arranged it. There, on the floor at the foot of my bed, sat my twenty-six year old daughter, her tongue peeping out the corner of her mouth in concentration. With a smile on her face and tears streaming down her cheeks, she was trying to gouge an opening in her wrist with a screwdriver. It was not working very well, but one had to make do with what one could find. I had hidden the sharp knives and ice pick before.

Looking up at the sound of my voice, she showed me her wrist. "See? Look! Pain. Pain?" Thinking I did not want my beautiful daughter scarred up any more than she was, I took the screwdriver from her, mentally consigning it to the general location of the knives and ice pick. Thinking I would like to know this little person before me, I leaned back and prepared to be acquainted.

"Yes, I see," I said in answer to her question, "Where is the pain?"

"In here," She said, pointing to her chest, "Please," She said, reaching for the screwdriver, "I need pain. Please. See? Pain."

118

Putting the screwdriver out of sight and out of reach, I asked another question. "What is your name?"

Smiling up at me through her tears, she informed me, "I am Anger."

"How old are you, Anger?"

"I do not know," she said, looking confused. "Younger than Pal!"

Not wanting to frighten her by asking what to her would be more difficult questions, I did not ask for information that is more detailed. I figured if my daughter, Lynn did not know Anger's age when she came back, (or did not know anger at all) I could ask Pal next time I talked to her.

"Where is Lynn?" I asked, as casually as I could. Still laughing and crying, she said with more confidence, "She is here watching and listening."

"Can Lynn hold you while you cry?" I asked, thinking this child needs to be cuddled and loved." Little Anger stated, "No, Mama always holds me when I cry."

So perhaps either Lynn is not ready for the responsibility of caring for this youngster, or maybe does not know her yet. "Do you want me to hold you?" I asked, holding my breath.

"Yes," she said, really crying now. As I held her, stroked her hair and made soothing noises, I thought back over the last few months. Lynn had always been a beautiful child who thought she was ugly. From an early age, I noticed she felt uncomfortable with children her own age. She seemed to gravitate toward adults and older young people who supervised her and who she could look up to, or young children, infants and toddlers especially. Children her own age intimidated her. This is still the case. Looking back, her careers of choice had always involved caring for the elderly or as a nanny for the very young, and they adored her.

Her brother-in-law once said, "She had everything going for her." If we had only known." We knew her grandfather as a young child had sexually molested her, but she seemed to be handling that better than most. Little did we suspect what was waiting just under the surface.

The waiting ended when her grandfather died. Now, we thought, we can put that behind us and get on with our lives. Not so, something like incest cannot be just swept under the rug without a trace. It stays there waiting for something to come along and kick the whole dirty mess out into the open.

Being raped by a so-called boyfriend was enough to do the job. All her old defense mechanisms swung into high gear. As a child, she could not fight her grandfather—that would be rude and besides he was bigger. She could not win. She could not run away. She was too small to make it on her own. Finally, she could not tell anybody. It was their secret and she had promised not to tell. Since she had to live with, eat with, play with him, and generally act as if everything was just fine, she had three ways out. She could kill herself, go crazy or escape mentally. Fortunately, she chooses the latter.

She created Pal, an eight-year-old friend who she could play with, eat with, sleep with and, when things got tough with Grandpa, share the pain, anger and fear with. She could just leave when she had all she could take and Pal would take over. The system worked so well that when another trauma happened (our divorce) she created another "person" to deal with the pain. Of course, this was all going on behind her back, so to speak, in her subconscious. She knew about Pal, but virtually all children have imaginary playmates, so she thought nothing of it. She did not know that Pal was a separate person with her own unique personality traits, her own memories, likes, dislikes, and so forth.

Rape, being a violation similar to incest, was the trigger that reactivated her old defenses. What was necessary for survival as a child, though, got in the way of dealing with stress as an adult. Instead of facing stressful situations and working out problems, she "escaped". Sometimes this resulted in her becoming a child again. Not herself as a child. She became another child—another person altogether.

As I held my daughter and rocked her I wondered, "How old is she?" Two perhaps? It would seem so. She did not speak in sentences until I asked her age. It must have frightened her so she went back inside. Four year olds are "younger than Pal" and can speak in sentences. Did she switch from a baby to a four year old? Possibly. This was all new to me. I could only follow my instincts the way mothers do and hope I said the right thing.

"Pain? Please, pain. I need pain here," Showing me her wrist.

"Why?" I asked.

"Because I am a bad girl. Grandpa says I am a bad girl. This is why daddy left. They say Grandpa is dead, but I do not believe them."

"I promise you Grandpa is dead." And none too soon for me, I thought, though I was careful to keep that sentiment out of my voice. This was a child, after all, whether she was two or four, and she loved him.

"Why?" she cried.

"Because he had a bad heart. He got sick and his heart stopped."

Then childlike, her attention shifted back to what

was important to her. "I did not make him stop. I am a bad girl. See? Pain. I need to blow my nose," she said abruptly.

While she was gone, I got back into bed and made room for her. Her feet were cold and she needed some warming up. She crawled into bed beside me and warmed her feet on mine. I lay quietly letting my mind wander over what I had just heard, thinking about things I had never had to dwell on before. Things like child abuse and pedophiles, knives, ice picks and screwdrivers. I heard Lynn's exclamation and turned to look at her. My daughter was back.

"Well, hello, there," I said.

She was looking at her wrist in dismay. "I did it again, didn't I? Is this the same person who used the ice pick?"

"No, this one just needed to feel pain. That one wanted to die."

In the next few months I was going to learn a lot about the mind and how it can defend itself from unbearable stress, be it physical pain or emotional. I came to be in awe of how, in a way I had never needed to be aware of, we are "wondrously made." We can remain sane under circumstances that are unbearable. If we are young enough at the time, we can choose to use the skill of "disassociation"—mentally go away until the danger has passed. This technique usually happens between the ages of birth to ten years old. <u>Repetitive</u> abuse or severe trauma occurs. This is when the child learns how to "go away."

Dissociative Identity Disorder (formally known as Multiple Personality Disorder or MPD) is a tool that was beginning to make sense to me. How many of us have experienced a desire to get out of a sticky or unpleasant situation? Just go. Leave. Maybe tomorrow things will be better. Isn't that what the old ostrich does? He sticks his head in the sand in hopes that when he raises his head and open his eyes, the danger will be gone. A person with Dissociate Identity Disorder goes him one better. She gets out. She leaves. Someone else steps into her shoes until the danger has passed. Handy is it not?

Sadly, these children are made, not born. They are made under conditions that should never happen to a child. These conditions must continue over a long period repeatedly, giving the child no chance to recover. We have known of children coming from satanic cults where sex abuse, physical abuse and human and animal sacrifice are the order of the day. They come from incestuous families where, if both parents are not abusive, then the one who is not is an enabler giving the child no escape.

As we learn more about this, and as it becomes more accepted by the psychiatric and medical fields, we may learn about another cause. Suppose it is no one's fault. No abuser. No cult. Think about the children who are in war zone. I have always wondered how they remain sane in the face of the horrors they are exposed to on a daily basis. There are your little cancer patients, burn victims—the list goes on. Each person is different, though there are enough similarities to enable as expert to make a diagnosis. In Lynn's case, it seems most of her "critters", as she calls them affectionately, remain at the age they were when they were created. They do not advance in age as some do. Pal, for instance, was created when Lynn was eight years old. That being the case, we only need to trace back to what was going on in her life when she was that age. However, it is not as simple as it sounds, and it takes time. Like gaining too much weight, this did not happen overnight. It will not just go away no matter how much you want it to. What happened, for instance when she was two? I do not know and Little Anger is so timid and so young that most of the time one of the older children tells us about her. Lynn has been in therapy for a year, now, and the incident with the screwdriver is the only time I have ever talked to her.

The only trauma I know of before age four happened when she was seven months old. She had been sick for four months. Her doctor had been unable to cure her—or diagnose her for that matter. She was losing strength and weight fast until at seven months she weighed less than her birth weight. I took her to another doctor. He diagnosed tonsillitis and ear infection and anemia he could only guess. Her DPT shot at three months? Maybe. We will never know for sure.

The one thing the doctor knew for sure was that the child was dying. He had to decide upon the best course of treatment for her without killing her. His final decision was to treat her as an outpatient. He feared that hospitalization at this stage would be more than she could stand. He started her on a regimen of penicillin—one shot a day for two weeks. Along with a diet change did the trick. By the end of this time, she could almost sit up by herself. It was quite a milestone. Then one shot every other day for two weeks. Then twice a week for two weeks. Then once a week for two weeks. At the end of this time, she was physically stronger. It was about this time that the doctor discharged her from his care. He told me, "I was not sure I could save this baby."

We have a picture of her sitting up at eight months old. Big sister was standing behind supporting her, but she was sitting! In a few more months, she was walking, talking, and generally healthy. Think about it from her point of view, though. Your mother, who is supposed to protect you from harm, takes you to this place full of strangers so some man can stick a needle into you—not just once. She keeps doing it for eight weeks. No wonder months later when we were driving by the doctor's office of a Sunday afternoon, I heard a scream from the back seat. Reacting the way most parents do, I asked Jane, her sister, "What did you do to her?"

"Nothing, Mom, I promise."

Upon asking Lynn what was the matter she screamed, "I do not want any doctor!"

Sure enough, there was the tall medical building on our left. I was shocked. It gave rise to some questions. Do young babies know what is going on in their world? Do they remember outstanding events the way we do? Obviously. Does Lynn have an infant in her inside family? It would not surprise me at all. Knowing that there is a two year old and a four year old who is "younger than Pal" gives us the clue that, by the time her grandfather got a hold of her at five, she was an expert at dissociation. Finding herself in an unpleasant or perhaps threatening situation, she could just leave. Tests at school, a scolding from her teacher or me would do it. It makes me wonder how many times, when I thought I was talking to my daughter, I was actually talking to someone I did not even know. So much pain Lynn was going through. It made me think of the Gods promise that one day there would be a world without tears.

A World without Tears

Just think of a world, a world without tears,
Where a man can live for a million years,
With never a grief, an ache, or a pain,
And never a thought of dying again.

Think of a world where a man plants a vine,
He can sit in its shade, and say, "This is mine."
He can live in the house his own hand made,
And naught shall molest, or make him afraid.

Think of a world without bloodshed and strife,
Where no man dare take another man's life.
Where man unto man will unite in peace,
And malice and hatred forevermore cease.

Think of the earth as a global paradise,
Where mountains and desert will dazzle your eyes
With beautiful flowers and shrubbery and trees
With gay butterflies, songbirds, and bees.

Think of a world where the beasts are all tame.
They won't hurt one another to kill or to maim.
Their fear of man gone, they'll no longer be wild.
Their leader will be a mere little child.

130

Think! Just as sure as God's word is the truth
A man shall return to the days of his youth.
His flesh shall become as the flesh of a child,
And the words that he speaks will be cheerful and mild.

Think of a world where a lame man will leap
From crag to crag like a deer or a sheep.
Where none will be deaf on none shall be blind,
And the dumb shall sing and speak forth their mind.

Think of a world where each man is his brother,
Not esteeming himself above that of another.
Where man unto man will be friend to friend.
In a world without tears, that will never end.

Think of a world where the dead will have risen
From their silent tombs that held them in prison.
To forever live to love and caress
Their loved ones and friends of righteousness.

Now a "World Without Tears." Is not just a dream
As many a person might make it seem.
For just as sure as the Bible is true
A world without tears now lies before you.

And since such a world before you now lies
Wouldn't you like to live in such paradise?
And share all the blessings that God has in store
For all who would do his evermore.

Good news of the Kingdom is still being sung

Throughout every nation, kingdom and tongue.
And all who are thirsting for truth are involved
To join the New World Society and be united.

In praising our God, our Savior and King
And giving to him all we have, everything.
That we might live throughout endless years
In a world without sorrow, "A World Without Tears."

"Watchtower Bible Tract Society Brooklyn New York."

"Isaiah 11: 6-9"

"Acts 24: 15"

Sometime 1984

The first of the telephone calls that I well remember I received at work. Lynn was in high school at the time doing very well some of the time and not so well the rest. The subject of the day was teen suicide and her teacher was someone that she trusted. The class was encouraged to come to him or an adult of their choice if they knew anyone who had talked about suicide. After class, she went to him and after talking with him for a while, he asked if he could call me. She agreed.

I came to the school hoping I was prepared to deal with whatever he was going to tell me and help my daughter. She did not need me falling apart in front of her. If necessary, that could come later when I was alone. She had been trying to kill herself, he said, by the simple process of not eating. She had been losing weight, but like everyone else in our family, she had always been slender, so a few pounds off just helped her look like the rest of us. My older daughter's weight fluctuates so much that she prepares herself by having what she calls a "fat wardrobe" and a "skinny wardrobe." Thus, she always looks nice and is resigned to the fact that, like the weather, her weight will change.

Lynn, on the other hand, was trying to kill herself. This was not as dramatic as slashing her wrist, but that would come later.

Thinking I was only dealing with one person that I knew (as much as any parent knows their teenagers); I set about trying to change her mind. Her teacher at school helped her from an academic point of view and became a father figure she so desperately needed. He was an adult male who, after three years in that school, she knew she could trust. His was an open door policy, and we will be forever in his debt. She could tell him things that she could not tell me. This could be things she was ashamed of, embarrassed about, school peer pressure and anything else she could not tell her friends (peers or adult) or me.

I, on the other hand was available to her at all other hours of the day and night. Some of our most intense conversations took place around one o'clock in the morning. These are the most valuable hours and I will always be thankful I did not waste them. These were times when she could not sleep and wanted to talk. (This is a most important ingredient since conversations of this nature need to be spontaneous, especially with the young).

We talked about everything under the sun. There were the topics of friends, family, school and her father, who was not active in her life at this time. He has since become a valuable person in her life and has helped her in therapy perhaps more than he knows. I hope their relationship will remain strong.

Besides my opinion on the matter, there was another strong lever I could use—her faith. She was convinced that the Bible is the Word of God, and she lived to please him. Being outwardly happy and a joy to be around, we had no idea how depressed she really was. Whether it was a physical chemical imbalance or psychological, it made no difference. It was very real and there was no talking her out of the opinion that living in this system, in this old world just was not worth the effort. Besides, if she could only die, God would resurrect her wouldn't he? Then—no more problems.

We had a friend who we shared a common interest with, and that was the love of horses. Lynn called her "Mama" at times. I shall always be grateful to our friend for being able to say the right thing at the right time. On hearing how Lynn felt, she turned to her and said, "Why should God resurrect someone who does not want to live in the first place?" Whether "Mama" was talking to Angie, Annie, Executioner or Lynn herself, it had the desired effect. She did not really want to die forever—just go to "sleep" until things got better. Now that dying was no longer an option, at least for Lynn herself, she set about trying to turn around and face life.

Unknown to us, however, this view was not shared by all of her inside people. Angie, for instance, uses starvation as a way of punishment for transgressions, real or imagined, especially when she is very depressed, or feeling a lot of pain inside. Annie thinks she is fat. She is anorexic and feels the less she weighs, the better she would look. Executioner, on the other hand, wants to die. He feels that is a way out and would put everyone's pain to an end. Lynn has had a hard time dealing with these three—especially before she knew, they were there. She has been in therapy for a year now, and they still get the upper hand sometimes.

Unknown to Lynn, her job through the years had been to hide her inside family. Their job was to protect her when necessary and secrecy was essential for them to be effective. Then her grandfather dies in the spring of 1992 and Lynn's guard dropped. Her inside family was exposed to a world they did not know, a religion they did not know or understood and people they had never seen.

Her inside family was getting stronger and braver because of being out more and their influence was being felt. Lynn, of course, knew none of this. Being co-conscious some of the time, she was able to tell us what went on when someone else was in control. She could not understand why she would do something that to her was unacceptable. It was like being a passenger in a car when the driver does not know how to drive. She could see and hear what was going on, but was not in control.

Some of the time, she was not co-conscious. This was an amnesiac barrier. It was a very useful tool during the abusive years and enabled her to act normal in the face of the horror that went on behind closed doors. Of course, you can imagine how frightened she must have been. To "come to" and have no idea how she got there or what she may have done while she was "out" was terrifying. I do not know which was worse, being out of control or just being "out."

Not knowing any of this, we were all puzzled and dismayed at her sudden irresponsible and bizarre behavior. She made new friends whose lifestyle and morals were diametrically opposed to Lynn's habits and values. Drugs, drinking, smoking and immoral sex were commonplace. Her inside family began to make decisions for her. Through these activities were not acceptable to Lynn, she was yet unaware of the existence of her inside family and was unable to oppose them.

Her inside family were so new to the world that they only knew the people Lynn had come to associate with after her grandfather died. They became accustomed to their ways and habits and made decisions according to their knowledge of what is acceptable. Lynn's old friends were strangers and they were afraid of them.

By late summer and fall, she was sure she was going crazy. If nothing else convinced her of this, the voices she was beginning to hear in her head did the job. She was crazy. She was a bad girl, just like her grandfather said. It was her fault her father left home when she was four. Grandpa had said so. She did not deserve to be happy. She hated herself, her association, and her behavior and yet was unable to change any of it. October 1992

When I received the second phone call, I was at work again. It was the middle of the night and Lynn was home alone. A police officer called, and after introducing himself, asked me, 'Was it you who hid the knives?"

Actually the answer was, "Yes."

During my last housekeeping, I had put the knives up on top of the kitchen cabinets. I had just wanted to make the counter look less cluttered and, since we did not use them daily, it seemed to be a good place for them. It had been eight years since her conversation with her high school teacher, but unknown to us her inside family was alive and well. She took some pills and, when she could not find the sharp knives, she settled for the ice pick.

She called 911 before permanent damage was done, but by the time they got to our home she had gone to work with the ice pick on her wrist. It was enough. She was in the hospital for a while and, when released, she was to see a counselor or therapist on a regular basis. She agreed. She was scared now and wanted to make sure this did not happen again.

Her first counselor saw her couple of times. Then during one session she asked, who else is with us other than Lynn?" Lynn's voice changed to what seemed like a child's voice and she said, "I am Pal."

"Where are you at Pal?"

Lynn pointed to the lamp off to her left. And said "Over there"

The counselor asked, "How old are you, Pal?"

"I am eight years old."

"Is there anyone else you can see?"

"I think I see a shadow lurking in the dark somewhere."

"OK," her counselor said, "We will call this figure you see Shadow. Is there anyone else you can see?"

"Yes," she said. "I see someone or something that is very angry."

"OK," her counselor says again. "We will call this one Anger."

Her counselor then assured her that she was not crazy, which she had begun to fear, and that this could be successfully treated. She was not experienced enough in this field, but she knew someone who was. It was the beginning of a long, rough road, but, even when she is very depressed, Lynn knows it is worth the trip.

One of the first steps we took at this time, after Lynn was diagnosed with Multiple Personality Disorder, was to tell the elders of our church what was going on. They had said she could talk to them anytime. They knew she was not well, but of course could not know what was really happening. In August it had been necessary to take harsher measures against her to keep the congregation clean from her sever misconduct. The emotional earthquake has just begun.

It was difficult for them to understand what we were saying to them. They had met Pal. They were talking to Pal when they told her of their decision. I imagine they found it difficult to understand why this young woman facing a judicial committee of elders can talk of nothing else but her chicken. I must admit I wondered about this myself. She continues in therapy and eventually when the time was right, about a year later, we got our answer.

Blackie was his name. Lynn had raised him from

141

a chick and he was tame. He was as tame as a kitten and loved to be held and carried around. I can still remember the joy he brought to her during their hours of play. He followed her around like a puppy and she loved him. He was a fair sized bird when Grandpa killed him. In front of Lynn, he broke one of his legs and then one of his wings. "We watched him flopping on the ground and screaming," Pal told me, crying. "I yelled at him to stop, but he would not." I held her tightly. "Why did he do it?" I asked her softly. "The night before I did not want to play his games. He said if I did not play his games, he would hurt me, too. Then he took a big stick and hit him. He hit him and hit him until his neck was broken and then he stopped making noises. He was dead. My Blackie was dead." I knew about him killing the little bird. It had been one of Lynn's first memories after starting therapy. We did not know about the torture, or the threat to her. Poor Pal. My heart ached for her.

"That is when I was created. That is my first memory. That is when Lynn created me. Then, after, he made me do awful stuff. I am a bad girl. I am such a bad girl."

"Why do you think you are a bad girl?" I asked, wiping her tears.

"Because I did not want to play his games. I was supposed to because he said to. But I did not want to, so I am a bad girl."

Then she dropped another bombshell.

"He said God wants me to play his games. He would pray to God with me and then play. That is why we do not want to go to the religious meetings. 'Cause God wanted me to play his games and I did not want to. That makes me bad. "

I explained to her, "God does not like those kinds of games."

Pal answers, "Grandpa said he did."

I told Pal, "Grandpa did not know God."

Pals reply, "He said he did."

I gently explained to Pal, "Grandpa was not one of Gods people. God was on your side. He does not like Grandpa's games, either."

Pal challenges, "You will have to prove it to me sometime."

I answer her by saying, "O.k. Remember in a

magazine we got today that has a lot of bible scriptures in it?"

Pal says, "Yes."

As Pal and I sat together, I read to her part of this magazine on "How Can We Protect Our Children?" It stresses that it is ok for a child to tell on an abuser. How Gods people in these religious meetings enforces moral laws. I helped her see that the blame falls only on Grandpa. Lynn (Pal) was a good girl. She and God wanted the same thing. Grandpa's actions were against Gods law. … ("It is the abuser and the abuser alone who bears the blame for the abuse.") "Awake pages 8, 10, and 14) "How Can We Protect Our Children?" "Watchtower Bible Tract Society, Brooklyn New York"

There was one man who had been kind to her recently –one of Gods people. He noticed her distress at one of the meetings one night and reached out to help her. Of course, he had no way of knowing he was talking to Pal or that Pal literally did not know him, but his kind words have helped her more than I can say. She is still afraid of God and his people—especially men, but she does not feel as threatened by them as she did before he spoke to her. Thinking of him, I asked her, "Remember the man who talked to you Thursday?"

Pal says, "Yes."

I explained to her, "He knows what Grandpa did."

"How did he find out?" Pal interrupted.

"Lynn told him a long time ago."

"Oh." Pal says.

"He was really mad when he found out. All of God's people hate what Grandpa did. That is why magazines like this are written, so we can learn how to protect our children." This conversation with Pal took place nearly a year after she was diagnosed and more than a year after she was dismissed from the congregation. It answered many questions for us. Why was the chicken so important? Why is Lynn so terrified at the meetings?

Yes, Pal has been there for her as a companion as well as a helper. She is one of Lynn's more dominant personalities because she has been out more, but we have to remember she is only eight years old. Naturally she is not going to act like an adult or think like an adult. She

145

does not know God. She knows who I am, because she told me once that sometimes when I would study the Bible with Lynn they, Pal and the others, would listen in. They, especially Pal, do not really want to know him because they believe what Grandpa said about him and are afraid. They are afraid God felt it was ok for Grandpa to play his games.

I cannot talk about spiritual things with Lynn, but I do with Pal and the others. Only one of Lynn's inside people is a dedicated, baptized Christian. She is the Pioneer, and she is upset. She did not do anything wrong. She did not even know about it, and here she is dis-fellowshipped. She helps me teach Pal and the others, though, and she has quite a job. There are twenty-six personalities altogether, and only three of them know God at all. If she will put her anger away and concentrate on teaching the other people who are available to her, she can happily pioneer for some time and not run out of Bible students.

The pioneer will have to be patient, though. One of these days Lynn will "get her ducks in a row," as her sister says and get reinstated. However, we have to wait until everyone else is ready. Being reinstated too soon would be like being baptized too soon. In the meantime, Lynn continues her therapy and the Pioneer and I try to help Pal, Shadow and the others get to know God. More, learn to trust him and his people—even grandfathers.

It was hard to convince everyone that Grandpa was dead. The children looked for him wherever they went. He had never lived in Portland, but, in the way of many young children, they had difficulty with distances not frequently traveled. I can remember young lynn when we would travel to Portland from eastern Washington. She knew that Portland was in Oregon, so in her mind, as soon as we crossed the Umatilla Bridge over the Columbia and into Oregon we should almost be there—in Portland. Therefore, after he died and Lynn's guard dropped they came out into a world that they thought was Richland. When we were in a crowd, Grandpa might be there. If he was not there then maybe he was outside mowing the lawn. Pal especially lived in fear of him. The reason for her fear was that Lynn had told on him. She had promised not to tell. He made it very plain what would happen to her if that promise were broken by demonstrating with Blackie.

When I raised my children, I can remember stressing that a promise is binding. If you promise anything, it must be carried out. If I had one thing to do over it would be to teach them that there are situations where you can break your word. For instance if an abuser forces a child to promise not to tell it is not wrong to break your promise. It is <u>never</u> wrong to tell on an abuser. They do not deserve your loyalty. They are in the process of betraying the child's trust, are they not? The child does not need to fight this war alone. In addition, I would define what abuse is. Touching where the bathing suit covers is a definition that a young child can understand. Anything that makes the child uncomfortable or afraid or causes pain is certainly abuse.

There was one way that she could be convinced that she was safe. We had to go to Richland to Grandpa's house and look for him. Look in the greenhouse, the trailer and the house and see that he is gone. She will need to talk to Grandma and Aunt Sue and Jane. This was going to be hard. There was the two-year-old Anger and four-year-old Cheryl who loves him. They are going to experience the grief and loss of the Grandfather they knew. Pal, although after of being alone with him, also loved him.

For this reason, we thought we would start with an easier one. One where there was no fear—no threat to them. We would start with Grandpa Don's death. They did not know he had died either. We would go to his grave and show the inside children where he is. We would talk about him, maybe, or cry a little. Our first visit was a short one. Harder for me, I think, than for Lynn. He was after all my father and I miss him very much. Her defenses were up and her children protected. Lynn herself was feeling very little grief. It was as if this was someone else's loved one. Therefore, we drove on that day and promised Sewry, the thirteen year old who loved him that we would come back soon.

We went back about six weeks later and this time Sewry was ready. She knew what to expect because of our first visit and was no longer afraid. She was also stronger because of being out more and because of her time in therapy. This was not going to be fun, but she could face it now and accept the truth that she had been denying for thirteen years. We sat beside his grave and talked to each other and to him. I held her while she cried and then we talked some more. Yes, Grandpa Don is dead, but we look forward to seeing him again in the future. We miss him, but it is no longer such an unbearable and permanent loss. Our memories of him are good ones and we can now enjoy talking about we would like to do with Grandpa when we saw him again.

It would be a long time, though, before Sewry would be able to let him go. To really be free of the flesh, raw grief that she had been created to endure. It would be a long time, also, before Lynn herself is ready to endure the emotions that she has been escaping from. When that happens we will come back to Sewry, but now, while she is working on this, others have memories and fears of their own to deal with.

Now we could make plans for our trip to Richland. Lynn's therapist and all her inside family began to prepare themselves. Since Mary Lu could not be with us, of course, she showed Lynn how to keep her children in their "safe place" and let the adults deal with it on this first trip. If this first trip went well, then Lynn would have a "support group" to help her take care of the children on succeeding trips.

Lynn's "safe place" is, of course, in her mind. It is a beautiful place now with a waterfall, a creek, the ocean, rocks for the children to play on, animals and a weeping willow tree. To one side of the tree is a fountain of "healing water." It was not always this way. Her people all used to live in darkness—a small windowless room where she could not see them and they could not see each other. They came out when they were needed and went back into the darkness when they went back inside. As Lynn progresses in therapy her "safe place" changes. There is a healing light from God now that The Peace Maker always stands in, and a rainbow. There is a graveyard where memories are buried once Lynn herself becomes strong enough to face and accept them. As this happens, one memory at a time, Lynn becomes stronger and can rely less on her inside family.

For this first trip, though, things were going to get ugly. No child should have to deal with what Lynn,

Pal and the others had gone through. Therefore, the children went into the safe place to play with Chameleon to care for them. Chameleon becomes just like the people around her and her accent changes too. (hence her name) and she likes children. She is a great help in caring for the little ones when Lynn or one of the older ones needs to relive a painful memory.

"Relive" is the word I have chosen to describe what happens. Lynn can actually see, feel, smell, taste, and hear in detail something that happened long ago. We "singletons" have experienced dreams as vivid on occasions, but in reliving or abreacting, as it is properly termed, a person is not asleep. Her mind goes back to an incident that happened long ago and recreates it. This is necessary to make the memory available to the core or original personality. In this case, the reverse would happen. We would make the fact that Grandpa is dead available to her inside family so they would no longer fear him.

We stopped off at Lynn's Uncle Lee's house. He and his wife, Sue, had invited us to stay with them. It was interesting to watch Lynn. Although Mary Lu had counseled her to stay in control as much as she could, it was not easy. It was not always possible. We were close to Grandpa's house now and everyone was scared. He could carry out his threats and maybe Lynn could not protect them. Blackie's memory was vivid and her fear was very real—not available to Lynn, yet, but the others knew.

Shadow was out more than anyone was. She does not trust people. She studies them as if she is committing each feature to memory, and maybe she is. She wears her makeup very thick to hide her identity. She is very mature and is the one who takes tests when Lynn is in school. Since she is an adult, she was not confined to the safe place with Chameleon.

It is disconcerting to know that Lynn's relatives are not related to her inside family. For instance, I am referred to as "Lynn's mom." Shadow does not talk any more than she absolutely has to, but on this first evening in Lynn's uncle's house she stated, "I do not want to go out there."

"Where?" I asked, though I was sure I knew.

"Out to that house," she said.

"Lynn's grandpa's house?" I asked.

"Yes. We do not want to hurt that woman. (Lynn's grandma) already knew about the abuse and was willing to do anything she could to help Lynn and all her family. It took some doing, but by morning Shadow, at least, was ready to go out there.

We visited with Grandma for a while and then, while I kept Grandma busy in the house, Lynn went outside to look around. Where to start? The trailer? No. Not yet. A small camping trailer was where most of the abuse took place. We were here so Lynn could convince her inside family that Grandpa cannot hurt them anymore. His threats cannot be carried out. He is dead.

At this, we had no idea of the lies Grandpa had told her. We knew about Blackie, but his threats went way beyond that. It was a good thing that Pal, especially, was in the safe place. She would not be ready to share those memories for a long time. Maybe the greenhouse. Grandpa was always puttering around in there. No, he was not there. She spent some time walking around the yard remembering the fun they had working together. It was a quiet time and pleasant, but suddenly she felt afraid. There was something wrong in the greenhouse and she ran.

We know now that this was where Blackie died. The details of his death were not available to her at this time. Besides this concerned Pal and she was with the other children in the safe place with Chameleon. We did not come here on this trip for memory recall or confrontation. Our only goal at this time was to establish the fact that he is indeed gone. They do not need to be afraid anymore. He cannot hurt them. The memory and confrontation would come at another time. We would make another trip after Mary Lu could guide her and prepare her for it. Right now, we were preparing the way—laying a foundation for further therapy.

While Grandma and I went grocery shopping, Lynn's father showed her where Grandpa's ashes were. I am not sure what all happened in there, but Lynn got a lot off her chest. She and Shadow told him what they thought of him in no uncertain terms and in general let a lot of feelings out so they would not fester under the surface any more. True, Grandpa was not there to hear, but saying the words she had long to say for so many years helped a lot. It exposed feelings Lynn did not know were there and there was material for many sessions with Mary Lu.

All in all, this entire first trip was a success. Lynn uncovered a lot of material she needed to get well, and a bonus was she found that other family members were not only interested but also supportive. They believed her and were prepared to help in any way they could. Lynn, Mary Lu and I were no longer alone. We had a support group that has been invaluable to us.

Surgery

In February 1993, Lynn got an invitation to go skiing. She had never been skiing before, though her friends had. With their encouragement, she skied too long—long after she was tired—and skied on the slop. Now, at Ski Bowl, when you go up on the lift there is only one-way down. I have been told that Ski Bowl is a lot of fun with level places and gentle slopes for beginners and cowards like me and steeper, longer runs for more advanced skiers. I would not know from personal experience, but it must be true. Ski Bowl is a popular place for skiers of all ages and skills. It is too bad her "friends" were not interested in whether she had fun or not—only themselves. They cared nothing for her safety and even urged her to try the long run. Of course, not wanting to ruin their day, she did.

Up the lift she went, losing one ski on the way and falling off the lift at the top, but she picked herself up and someone brought her ski up for her so everything seemed to be in order. Off she went, and they were right. It <u>was</u> fun! It was like flying. Down, down, faster and faster, but also like flying sometimes landing is the hard part. Trying to slow down and turn, she heard a noise "Like Rice Crispies", she said. Her body and right leg went one way and her left lower leg went the other, bending sideways at the knee. She came down to the lodge in a snowmobile. They wrapped the knee and cared for her. Her "friends" went back up to ski some more. They thought she was faking it to get out of skiing anymore.

Looking back with 20/20 hindsight, she knew she should have quite sooner. She knows she should not have tried the long run, but peer pressure was too strong and pleasing her friends was more important to her than her own safety. As in other pressure situations in her life—just do it. She is curious to know what it feels like to speak her mind. What is it like to feel confident enough in her own self to value herself? How does one learn to say "NO?" "NO" in such a way that there will not be any abusers because the would-be abusers will know she means what she says, and will leave her alone. It will be an about-face for her, but maybe if Pal is growing up and maturing, that will take care of itself

158

with practice. Maybe then, she can move up in the pecking order.

Time passed. Months in physical therapy showed a marked improvement in the knee. She worked hard and I helped her with her exercises at home so the range of motion was back to normal, but there was still marked weakness there and a possible torn ligament. Since she was so young, the decision was made to go ahead with surgery to find out for sure the extent of the damage. If she needed reconstruction with the ligament, well, that would just have to wait. Meanwhile they would take care of the little stuff and hope that would be enough.

We had an interview with the surgeon who explained what he was going to do, complete with pictures, so we would know what to expect. Then an interview with her anesthesiologist was scheduled. We wanted him to know she had Dissociative Identity Disorder. Different alters respond differently to the anesthetic and /or pain medication. What would be proper for Lynn may be too much for the inside children or not enough for one of the adult alters in her system. He needed to know.

159

He was wonderful to her. Obviously, he had other patients with this disorder and knew what to expect and how to handle any eventuality. He explained the routine in detail. This included the time they expected her at the hospital, when surgery was scheduled and everything that would happen in between. Then he turned to me and asked, "Would you like to be in the surgical recovery when she wakes up?" I was shocked. Nobody is allowed in the recovery room. There is too much going on and family members are only in the way. Besides, when people come out of surgery they are not pretty with all those tubes and things. I could be nearby if they needed me, but I was not expecting this. He went on to explain, "The person who goes under anesthetic is not always the person who wakes up."

I had not thought of that, but it made sense, sure, I would be there if he thought it be best for her. He did. He wanted whoever woke up to see a familiar face. One who could tell the nurses if the patient is not Lynn.

Lynn wanted to know why she had to come to the hospital so early. Two hours seemed like a long time to her. He had explained everything earlier right up to the pill she would take to make her sleepy and other preparations to be made, but either someone else had been "out" for a while or Lynn was not paying attention. Either way, she had a question, so I tried my best to answer.

"You have to get here, get out of your clothes and into bed, take your oral medication, give it time to work, and...." Poof!

I took another looked. Pal was frightened. She was wringing her hands and trembling. She started to look for an escape when I said sharply, "Lynn!"

She blinked a couple of times, put a hand to her head and then looked at me. "Lynn?" I asked.

"Yes, I am ok." Lynn was back.

We thanked the anesthesiologist for his kindness and understanding and at his suggestion; we went down to the admitting office to pre-admit.

As we were waiting outside the office I asked, "What upset Pal?"

"What do you mean?" Lynn asked

"Pal was out up there. She seemed frightened."

This was one time Lynn was not co-conscious and had lost the time Pal was out.

Lynn asked, "What was happening when she came out?"

"I was telling you what would happen between the time you get here and the surgery itself."

"What exactly did you say?" Lynn asked.

I went through the list and when I got to "oral medication" Lynn said, "Oh." She looked uncomfortable and more than a little embarrassed.

"Pal cannot stand the word "oral." It makes her sick. She gags and throws up when she thinks of it." She looked at me sideways, hesitated, and then went on. Because of what Grandpa did. She even has trouble brushing her teeth."

I was not expecting this, but it made sense. Therefore, we do not use the word "oral" any more. We use "pill" or "capsule" or "liquid", but not "oral". She will tell me when it does not bother her anymore.

The day for surgery came and the operation went without a hitch. Accept for the fact that this surgery was supposed to be a same day surgery. Lynn was supposed to go home the same day when it was all over. Lynn was starting to wake up and she began to complain about pain in her knee. Therefore, the Doctor gave her a pain medication called Dilaudid and back to sleep she went. The nurses could not get her to wake up. She went into a coma like state. She had to spend the night under observation.

Lynn tells me that during her deep sleep, she could hear everyone around her but she could not move or open her eyes. She heard the doctor say, "We cannot let her go home like this. She has to stay overnight." Lynn also heard the nurse keep saying her name repeatedly. Lynn even recalled feeling the nurse putting the pulse rate monitor on her bald toe. The toe with no toenail. She mentioned how badly she wanted to laugh about this but could not move at all. This just proves to show that people in a coma can at times hear and feel everything around them.

When Lynn was starting to wake up again the next day, they called me in and it was Lynn herself. The surgeon came to tell us that the ligament was stretched, but not torn. No future operations would be necessary.

Now it was up to her and physical therapy. She is still working on it and will be for some time.

It is good to know that this disorder is beginning to be accepted by the medical profession and they are learning that medicating these people can be tricky. They are working on it, though, and I am glade. This condition is very real and a larger percentage of the population have it than has been previously thought.

December 1993

Resistance

"I do not want to go see Mary Lu today. It is just a waste of money. I have nothing to talk about today. Everything is going just fine. I have no problems. Why waste my money and her time?" These statements and more I have been hearing lately, even to, "I would not go see Mary Lu today except you want me to."

Why? Why, after all these months of looking forward to therapy and viewing
Mary Lu as the one person in the world she could trust, is she now trying to avoid her? We can only keep going one day at a time and wait for the answers.

Also bothering her are dreams that disturb her sleep.

1) Lynn needing a friend's help because she is hurt and bleeding, but the friend wants to go find the "skateboarders."

2) Lynn in bed. I am in the kitchen typing. Lynn is dreaming she is asleep. She sees spirit-like creatures coming towards her from the front

and from both sides. As she watches, the creatures come together in front of her and become one.

Possibly, she is getting ready to integrate. This frightens her for many reasons. One, she has never been whole before that she can remember. We are all afraid of the unknown. Two, she also has many questions like, what is it like to not care what other people think? What is it like to be in control? What is it like to be a singleton? What is it like to be confident—not to be afraid to speak your mind? What is it like not to be a pretender? She has given up or lost many things this past year. Among them are all her old friends that she loved dearly, her former relationships—in short everything and everyone that she held dear. Now, if she integrates, she will lose the only person of value that she has now—Mary Lu. She (and her alters) do not want that to happen, and it will if she gets well—a real catch twenty-two.

I have seen her under pressure. Not too long ago a person she respected forced her to do something she had never done before. She could not get away from

166

him. Therefore, to make him stop verbally abusing her she used the only tool she could think of. She lied to him. She told him what he wanted to hear. It worked like a charm. I was amazed that a person as intelligent as he is could be so easily deceived. Nevertheless, because it was what he wanted to hear, he believed her. As long as she was telling the truth, he pushed back verbally even though Lynn was agreeing with him. It was not until she lied to him that he was satisfied. Of course, by the end of the conversation he was not talking to Lynn any more. He was talking to Pal. Her only defense is to give the abuser what he wants.

After a lifetime of reacting in this way to pressure from other people you can understand why she has the questions she has. What is it like to be a person? She will be pleasantly surprised, but it will be different. She will feel alone and maybe lonely with nobody to "talk" to, but her life is just beginning. It is an exciting time—a time I do not want to miss. To be able to watch my little girl mature into a woman should have taken years. I will get to watch the process in months, maybe weeks. It has been a long time coming and I have often wondered what was holding up the process. Now I can be grateful that she had the skills to survive and become a mature, undamaged adult.

We went to a religious meeting in November, Pal got upset and so we left early. As we talked together, she said to me, "Why did Grandpa do that to me when I was a little girl?" Well, now last I knew Pal was still a little girl. On the other hand, was it Pal who was asking the question? Is Pal growing up? It will be interesting to see. Maybe I will ask her next time I talk to her. She was too upset or I would have asked her then. I am looking forward to another visit.

Lynn's "safe place" has changed lately, too. It is misty and foggy and things are difficult to see. The Peace Maker is the only one under the healing light. The others are afraid of the truth. Negative feelings and opinions about her have become the norm. These thoughts are not tolerated under the healing light because they are not true. Hence another change. She has to feel good about herself when under the light and she is not used to that. Blaming herself for her parent's divorce is one example. The attitude has become an integral part of her personality. She believes she is stupid and ugly. Anything that goes wrong in her life or in the lives of anyone around her is all her fault. Of course, this is not true, but it is the legacy of her grandfather who told her so, and she believes him.

December 25, 1993

"Lynn, how old is Pal?"

"Let me think. Eleven—she is eleven years old now."

"So she is almost the same age as Cheryl who is 12?" I find it interesting how there are three Cheryl's at different ages.

"No. The Cheryl's are still very young, the long legged eleven-year old I see playing with our German Shepard is Pal...I think."

"Do you want me to ask her next time I talk to her?"

"Yes. You will get the truth from Pal. She tells it like it is."

This is true unless you doubt her word and try to make her change her story. Then, in defense, she will tell you what you want to hear. I am looking forward to the next meeting we go to together. Pal is the main one to come out at religious meetings, if I can gently guide the topic of conversation around to ages of different alters or to growing up, I may find an opportunity to ask her. On the other hand, Pal just may tell me. She listens in on conversations I have with Lynn and if she has something on her mind, she comes out with it. She may be happy she is growing up or she may be worried about the change. Either way it is something she may want to talk about.

December 27, 1993

"Who is out?" I asked one day.

Lynn was sitting on the couch, rocking. She was not looking at me or talking. Very quietly, she sat and rocked.

"The Quiet One," she said.

"It has been a long time since I have talked to you."

"Well," Lynn's voice said, "I am talking for her."

The Quiet One seldom talks, hence her name.

She is ten years old—the age lynn was when we met my father, "Grandpa Don. Less than a year later, while she was still ten, we moved away from Richland and Grandpa. Also away from the rest of the family, she loved so dearly—her Grandma, aunts, uncles, cousins, and her sister. So here, we were here in the city with my father. She really missed the rest of her family and friends she left behind.

The Quiet One is afraid of people. I cannot recall Lynn was particularly timid at that age, but it was a year of change. From the country to the city. From her father's family to mine. From a large extended family to a very small one. No wonder the Quiet One is quiet. She has nothing to talk about that would interest her new city friends.

"Pal wants to come out. I can feel her in my head," Lynn's voice went on, though she was still rocking and looked like the Quiet One.

"Alright," I said.

"You wanted to talk to me."

It was not a question. Evidently, she had been listening during the past few days.

171

"Who is out?"

"I am Pal."

Sure enough the rocking had stopped.

"How is everyone?"

"We are scared. Lynn is sad. We are afraid to go to meetings and that makes Lynn sad. We were doing so well until that old man looked at us through Grandpa's eyes. Until he pointed his finger at us and said, we were bad. We know that, but he did not have to nag and nag. We do not want to go those meetings with all those old men. Especially that one. He is mean."

"You do not have to talk to him, and he will not talk to you until Lynn asks him to."

"He had better not. If we have to talk to those three men, again it will be under one condition, he will not point his finger at me and tell me how bad I am, if he has something to say he can just say it and that is enough. He does not have to go on and on like that."

The three men Pal was talking about were the elders in the congregation that had been trying to help Lynn turn her life around in as loving of a way as possible. They cared a lot about Lynn and wanted to help as much as they could. However, all Pal could see was older men that were saying she was bad when they really were not.

I assured her, "I am sure that can be arranged. That is not Grandpa you know."

Pal says, "Oh, I know that, but he looks at me through Grandpa's eye's."

I looked at "that old man" again the next time I saw him and I could see the similarity. The glasses are what did it. The eyes are similar. Though this man only wants to help her and not abuse her, the glasses make him look at her "through Grandpa's eyes." That is not his fault, of course, but not Pal's fault either.

After a pause Pal said, "I am bigger, you know."

"Are you? How big?"

"The long—legged one playing with our German Sheppard is me."

"How old are you know?"

"I am about eleven. Grandpa Don is here too. He has not got sick and died yet."

Yes, he died when Lynn was thirteen and got sick a year before that.

173

"I am taller now and my hair is longer. I am not as ugly as I use to be."

"You always did like long hair." I said to her.

"Yeah…The little Cheryl's are not together any more, you know. They split apart again. They are Daddy's girls, you know. I think there is something wrong there with Lynn's Dad. They really miss him."

"Maybe they can call him on the phone and talk to him." I suggested.

"Oh, he is deaf. He cannot hear anything without his hearing aids," she said scornfully.

"You know, maybe we can get him one of those attachments to put on his phone that would make your voice louder so he can hear." I suggested.

At her puzzled look I added, "There was a lady who used to live where Lynn works that had one on her phone. It worked really well for her and she was very deaf."

"I do not know…maybe. You know he never did keep his promise. He was going to take us fishing and he never did."

Pal looked enthused for the first time and said,

"Now that is something I can really do! I like to go fishing."

"Well, we will get that attachment for Lynn's dad's phone and maybe this next year you two can get together. Also you could write him a letter."

"Probably. You know Jane is a lot like Shadow. She really is. Shadow is Jane. I just thought of that this minute. Shadow is Jane. I always wanted to be like Jane and Shadow is Jane. I always loved her so much and wanted to be like her, but Jane would not let me get close. She would not let me be her friend."

Thinking about it makes sense. Jane is nearly seven years older than Lynn, and as children, the seven-year span made it nearly impossible for them to be friends. Jane does not trust people and neither does Shadow. For as long as Lynn can well remember Jane has worn makeup, and like Shadow, only a select few are allowed close to her. Oh, she is friendly enough and most people like her, but only a select few are allowed to see the real Jane. It is possible that Lynn (Pal in this case) has never felt that she was one of the few.

In creating Shadow, perhaps Lynn felt that here

175

is a "Jane" that she can get close to—be friends with. However, like Lynn and Jane, Lynn and Shadow are too different to be friends. Lynn has never been allowed to see the real Jane, and in the same way, she has never seen shadow clearly. Shadow wears a cloak with a hood that keeps her face in the shadows and heavy makeup to hide her identity. Also like Jane, Shadow is a dependable force and can be depended upon to handle any situation you could name, but she will not be used or abused—not even by Lynn. Like Jane, Shadow is her own person and is only there when she wants to be. However, in an Emergency situation or when someone needs her, both Jane and Shadow are there to help.

"I do not want to grow up. It scares me. I do not want to integrate either. That is like dying and I do not want to die. I thought people were mean when I was little, but the bigger I get the meaner people get. Like those friends of Lynn's. They have no right to be mad at us. Lynn apologized for whatever she did wrong to them after all."

"You know," I said, "When you get bigger you can have more say in who you associate with. You do not have to be friends with everyone—only the ones you choose. You can leave the rest alone. Associate with the ones who are not mean to you."

"Am I bigger? I mean do I sound different?"

"You use bigger words. I can still tell that it is you, but you do not talk like such a little girl."

"Oh. I am tired. I do not want to integrate. If I get well I will lose you."

"How will you lose me?"

"If I get well you will not be able to associate with me."

"Why not?" I asked Pal.

"Because Lynn is dis-fellowshipped and you cannot talk to dis-fellowshipped people,"

"Wait a minute," I said. I got up and sat beside her. "What happened, happened when you were not well and Lynn was not in control. We have to look at the reason for dis-fellowshipping. In some cases, it is to keep the congregation clean and punish the person that will not turn their lives around. They refuse to listen to Biblical counsel and willfully not change at all. Lynn needed to realize the hard way that what she was doing was very wrong and needed help to see that. She needed to be motivated to get well so that what she was doing repeatedly would not happen again. But she did not decide to do wrong things to turn away from God."

"Oh, we did not do that." Pal says.

"I know. So do the elders. Besides, does it make sense that I would walk beside you all this time and then, as soon as you are well, to abandon you? You will have to do the leaving. You will have to tell me to take my religion and shove it if that is what you want."

"You will not leave?" Pal asks.

"No, I will not leave; even after you are all well I will be here."

December 28, 1993

Twins

Therapy is moving right along. Resistance is still strong. Lynn says that every time she sees Mary Lu now something happens. She has even told me she is afraid of Mary Lu. Today was no exception. I can understand her fear, though I do not pretend to know how she feels. We are all afraid of the unknown, though, and what is happening now is exciting, but untraveled territory.

Pal is afraid to integrate, afraid of getting well and growing up. I can only wonder if the others feel the same way. Maybe this is the core of her fear. She seems timid and unsure of herself in everyday life, also. Afraid of everything from religion to the workplace. Thinking about it, it seems to involve structured atmospheres where there is acceptable and unacceptable behavior. The unacceptable carries severe penalties from dis-fellowshipping on the one hand to being fired on the other. Not that remaining on the "straight and narrow" is so difficult. It is just that the threat is there like a specter on her shoulder. Like Grandpa with Blackie. "Do what I say or else."

It is not easy for me to keep my mouth shut. The temptation is to treat her as an adult, but I have to remember that at times she is thinking and feeling like a child. The children may not be out, but their influence is felt. If Pal is feeling threatened, maybe the other children are also. Feelings influence our behavior more than we would like to admit, and feelings are definitely close to the surface now. Feelings have been suppressed all of her life, and she is only just learning to cope with emotions good and bad without escaping and becoming someone else. It is a very new experience for her, and, like a child going through adolescence, learning to cope with and control her emotions is not easy. Mary Lu said not to be surprised if she acts like a teenager. Evidently, this unstable period is to be expected in the same way the rest of us have gone through a similar period, usually in our teens.

Today Lynn brought a picture to show Mary Lu. It is a picture of a beautiful Indian maiden. She says it looks just like The Peace Maker. They were talking about her and her function in the system when suddenly Sherry's face showed amazement. Excited discovery, also.

"What is it?" Mary Lu asked.

"It is Shadow," Lynn said excitedly. "Shadow has removed her cape and hood and I can see her! I can see what she looks like!"

Shadow had never revealed herself until this day. Remember, she has always kept her face covered to hide her identity.

"They are twins!" She told Mary Lu. "Shadow and the Peacemaker look exactly alike. Is it possible to have twins?"

"Yes," Mary Lu told her. "It is very possible."

Did she create The Peace Maker because Shadow is too much like Jane? Pal said Shadow is Jane. Yet Lynn wanted and evidently needed a Jane she could be close to—be friends with. A Jane she could love without feeling intimidated. A Jane who would love her back— and show it. The Peace Maker is just such a person. Jane shows the strength like Shadow, and the gentleness and the love like The Peace Maker. What a beautiful combination her sister is. It will all come together and all questions answered when Jane is ready. In the meantime, she has to stay in therapy no matter how frightened she is. She has to keep in mind that, though this is one of the rough spots in the road to health and happiness, it is worth the trip.

March 10, 1994

Pal

"Ann, can you come up now?" Mary Lu's voice came down the stairway. I went up the stairs and Mary Lu was waiting for me. "We have Pal here today," she said. There was Pal sitting in the chair by the window.

"We have a problem here I am not sure how to solve. I know you do not celebrate birthdays, but is there some way that is acceptable to you that you can celebrate an important event? Pal has grown up and no one noticed. She would like to have a party and invite all the others in the system. Can this be done?"

"Oh, yes," I said. "We celebrate graduations, weddings and other important events, yes; we can have a party for pal."

I turned to Pal. "What would you like to do?"

"I want to have a party," she said. "I would like to climb trees or go horseback riding. Maybe play with snakes or spiders," she laughed. "I want to invite all the others, though, and they would not like that. Especially Shadow—she does not like snakes and stuff like that. So we will leave them home."

183

She looked at me mischievously and said, "I have a frog, you know? I found him one day on a log in the stream. That is why I have not even told Lynn about him. His name is Sam."

"Maybe we can leave Sam home, then."

"Yeah, I want to do something everybody likes to do. Remember that watch we saw earlier?"

"Yes." We had seen a watch at a department store that she would like, but the store employee was talking on the phone and would not wait on us, so we had left. Fortunately, it was one of the bigger chain stores, so I said, "There is another store that is like it here in town. We will go see if they have one like it."

"I hope so. I want something pretty. We all use the body and this is something we all could use. Lynn could use it at work and everything. In addition, some shoes. We need some shoes."

Well, if you are going to hit Mom up for a party and a present, you might as well strike while the iron is hot. Who knows? You might get it.

Mary Lu helped her get Lynn back and we left. It was not as nice of a party as I had planned because the car broke down, but we got other transportation and then went shopping. She got her new watch and shoes. I was going to take her out for pizza, but it was getting late so we stopped at a hot dog stand for a quick supper. As we sat and ate our meal we visited. Lynn was "out", but Pal was there, too, obviously enjoying herself.

I was amused at myself at the ease with which I was learning to "switch" with her from one personality to another. It was similar to the ease with which I switched in early years when our family was together. When I spoke to my husband, it was to an adult. With my oldest daughter, seven years older than Lynn, I spoke in language she could understand. Lynn was a baby, and there were always children of all ages coming and going. The only difference now is that I am talking to different people of different ages, sexes, likes, dislikes and opinions—all encased in the same body. A year ago, they did not accept me as their mother and they had yet to learn to trust me. Now Lynn told me something that touched me deeply.

"I have to tell you something, Mom."

"What is it?" I asked.

"Pal was too shy to tell you herself, but she wants me to tell you she loves you. She wants to call you Mom."

I was absurdly pleased. To think I was being accepted to that extent by a girl who had been betrayed and abused more than any of the others was a milestone indeed. She had no reason to trust anyone, yet here she was offering me her love and trust. I must be careful with this gift, I thought. Never let her down in any way, even by accident.

It was quite a "grow up party" indeed. Pal was excited and proud to be hosting a party for all her friends to come and enjoy. We all enjoyed the time together and of course, Pal was excited and pleased with the watch and the shoes. It was I, though who had received the greatest gift of all. **********

Healing

The mystery of who I was and why I did the things I did began to unravel. The wrong choices I had been making and could not avoid them. Friendships came and went some good and some bad. I always had felt so lonely when in reality I was never alone. I was only tricked in thinking I was all alone in my mind. I had to learn the hard way that I did not need a man or a husband and I did not need to be a mom to feel complete.

I had my mom, my sister, and everyone else that loved me in my family. To have one or two true friends were more important than a dozen so called friends. However, sometimes it takes losing everything in your life to realize what you truly had was good all along. The alters continued to run my life and I still had thoughts of death.

As I was sitting alone drinking my beer and smoking my cigarette, I planned to end my life for the last time when I got home from the bar. This time I would end it right. I was completely done being used and abused. A friend came over saying, "Hi Cherokee, how is it going?"

I wore my Indian jewelry every time I went out. Hence, the nick name "Cherokee", I told him that I was stood up. Then as I looked over his shoulder, I saw a very nice looking man standing across the bar. I told Chuck that I was going over to that man over there and I am going to say hi. I knew I would never see this person again and all I wanted was to just have fun and then go home and follow through with my plan.

Chuck smiled and said, "You go right ahead and do that Cherokee."

Little did I know that Chuck knew him and that they were very good friends. Therefore, I did just as I said I would. I went over to him and politely asked, "What is your name?"

He smiled and answered, "Bill."

I told him that my name was Cheryl. I went by Cheryl instead of Lynn as a way of starting my life all over. Fresh and new, starting with my name.

I asked him, "Do you want to go dance."

He shrugged and said, 'Yes."

Again, I knew I had nothing to lose and I would never see him again so in a joking sort of way I asked, "Can I do whatever I want to do to you?"

Knowing I was just kidding around we both laughed. I just wanted to relax and enjoy the night. Soon after that, we found ourselves at a table talking the night away. He was depressed over wrecking his car the day before and I was depressed about being stood up. We were good company for one another. After having breakfast, I went to work that same morning. We began to date and he never once stood me up. I was 103 lbs when I met Bill. I was slowly dying of anorexia and I did not care.

Four months later on July 4, 1995 I was at work, felt very sick, and did not know why. Then it dawned on me that I had not had my monthly cycle yet this past month. I took a test and found out that I was going to be a mom. I weighed 106 lbs and I looked very hard at myself in the mirror and said, "You better get well as of now." This meant I had to start eating and start being responsible. I most certainly was not alone now.

I continued to meet Mary Lu and she was

worried about me having a baby and not being integrated yet. My mom was very worried also, I tried to completely integrate but it does not work if you force it. Therefore, I did the best that I could do. Bill and I got married November 11, 1995 and we lived with his mom. This was one of the most challenging times of my life because the only person I have ever lived with was my mom. Now I was living with a man, his mom, and about to have a new baby. The adjustment was not easy for any of us. I needed a great deal of help from Mary Lu during this time of my new life.

I had my son February 17, 1996. It was a very difficult pregnancy. I had kidney failure when I was seven months along and my baby and I almost died. They put a stint in to open the urethra that leads to the kidney. Nevertheless, as you can see we survived. It meant many needles and The Pretender helped me through the sudden changes in my life as well with the needles while being pregnant. The Pretender helped me appear that I was doing well and that I was happy. My mom and Mary Lu knew differently. I was slowly losing control and feeling as if I was going to have a nervous breakdown while I was living with my Mother-In-Law. I was in a strangers house and living with my new husband and was about to have a new baby. My son was 7 pounds 5 oz. 19 inches long. He was something of my very own and I was very proud to have him in my life.

Time went by and soon I had to receive some depressing news. Mary Lu was retiring and I was about to lose her. What were we going to do now? What am I going to do without her help? We were grieving inside and now very scared. I knew I would not see anyone else and that I was now on my own. She taught me so much in how to survive any challenges I may have to face. The foundation had been made and I had a very good chance getting through life better than I had ever before. I will forever be grateful to her for all her successful and hard work.

I did my best being a wife and a mother. There were times I did not make good choices in how to handle conflicting circumstances between Bill and me. It felt like the way I treated my good grandpa, was the way I was treating Bill. The only men I knew was ones that abandoned me or abused me. The acceptation to this rule was my Uncle Lee and Uncle Steve. However, they did not have the "Grandpa" title and I knew them my whole life. Therefore, when good men came into my life and I did not know them very well I did not know how to act. It was both a struggle and a challenge. Bill and I eventually moved out on our own and succeeded in handling tough situations together. We did not let these challenges tear us apart.

Four years later, I had a little girl. My daughter was born March 10, 2000. She was 6 lbs and 10 oz. 20 inches long. By this time, we lived in our own home in Woodland WA. Now I had two reasons to get well and be strong to the best of my ability. They have both seen me switch. One day I was so upset with something and I was in the bathroom talking to myself. I know we all have this tendency, however, I answer back. My son walked by and said, "Mom you are doing it again!" He just shook his head and smiled. I snapped out of it and smiled back. Their love is unconditional and I love both of my kids for that.

The alters are still strong and active. I do not know how Bill gets through it some days. Annie is always lurking around the corner. I am constantly struggling with the thought "I am fat." Someone inside is a cutter. The cutter I am sure is Violet. The cuts are deep scrapes to distract me from the depression and the inside pain I feel. However, Bill helped me see that this is very unhealthy and to knock it off. Therefore, I have. I no longer cut. Violet realizes that her actions could cause me to lose my husband and children. I finally have a healthy relationship and a family. She will not be the cause of me losing them. She sees they are good and does not want us to lose them.

I think of death a lot and still wonder if everyone would be better off without me. It is so easy to think only of my pain and how I want to get away from it all. I do not think of what my death would do to the ones that I love so much and would leave behind. When we do this, we need to keep in mind what it would feel like to us if someone we love very much died. It is one thing when an elderly person dies such as a Grandpa or a Grandma. Because we can say and look back and know, they lived their lives to the fullest. However, what would it do to my family if I died at such a young age? How would they feel? What would they go through if I took my own life? What of the guilt and pain I would leave them while I selfishly am asleep in death.

Then it happened. December 29, 2006. 10:30 pm. I was watching TV with my husband Bill when the phone rang. We let the answering machine get it. It was my Uncle Howard.

He said, "Lynn it is Uncle Howard. Call back. It is an emergency."

I called him back. He stated, "Allan died tonight. "No not my cousin Allan, Oh God no"

I asked, "How did it happen?" Uncle Howard told me that he had died from a tragic accident while trying to help another driver that was involved in a wreck. While administering first aid, a truck came around the bin very fast and almost hit Allan. He jumped over the railing thinking he was going to land safely on the other side and ended up falling fifty-four feet to his death. Some people say that, "Time stands still for no one." Well on this fateful night, it felt like time stood still for a very long time. It was as if I was moving in slow motion and a part of me died with him.

I called my sister Jane and told her, "Jane, our Allan has died. He is gone Jane. Our Allan is gone." All she could say was, "Damn."

I cried so hard that night I thought my head was going to blow up. The pain was unbearable. It would not go away. I was switching repeatedly. Pal was so scared and upset. Allan was her best friend along with my other cousin Mae as young children growing up. Allan's funeral day had arrived. I walked into the church. As I was walking us front so I could share my feelings about Allen to everyone that attended I saw him lying in his casket. Pal was not prepared that there was going to be an open casket ceremony. I froze. It felt like I was on the other side watching from the inside. I guess you could say all the alters were traumatized by his death.

The grieving lasted for two years straight. I could not function without crying almost every day. Bill finally said, "Cheryl, (this is what Bill called me and the rest of my family called me Lynn.) You have to start living for your family now. Stop grieving for Allan. He would not want you to stop living because he died." He continued saying," What about us? We need you."

I had pictures up of Allan sitting up in my dining room and it was so painful to look at them. My son knew this and said, "Mom I want you to take down Allan's pictures."

I asked, "Why?"

"Because it makes you sad and I do not want you sad anymore."

I took down his picture and said goodbye. I still feel the loss to this day. It made me think of how painful a young loved ones death really is. It dawned on me that this is what I would be putting my family through only worse. Allan's death was an accident; mine would be by my own hands. Life is worth living no matter how much pain or depression you feel. My Grandpa Don use to tell me, "Every day is a good day when you can wake up to see the sun rise." I lived with hating to see another day because to see another day meant to feel more pain.

We get so use to feeling the bad we forget to see any good. If you can make a list of all the good things, you have or like about yourself and make a list of all the bad stuff, let us say there was only one good thing and a thousand bad, which do you think would be worth living for and grow on? That one good thing to me was that I only liked my eyes. I did not even see my mom or sister in the picture I was so depressed about my life. All I could think about was myself and did not consider anyone else. How selfish this was now that I think back. However, I liked my eyes. Therefore, I worked on that one good thing, soon the list got bigger, and I was able to see the bigger picture, which were my mom and my sister. I now see Bill, my son, my daughter, and my nieces and nephew. This list began to get so big of good stuff I could have gone on forever. Nevertheless, that took time and a lot of work that was well worth the effort.

After Allan's death and I felt that raw pain of losing him, I began to see my kids and family in a completely new light. I began to live and feel again. There are steps that I have taken and they are, "Remember the good or bad once again, start to feel once again, deal with the pain, grieve, and start to heal to love once again." We have to start by remembering then start feeling, deal with the pain so we can grieve which leads to healing which leads to forgiving then we can feel the love and joy life truly has to offer. Through all the mud and muck we may be going through, love and joy is there waiting for you.

Remember when you keep the anger and pains locked up inside, you are the only person that you are hurting. You are not hurting the one who has hurt you in the past. We all have the power to say to our abusers face to face or in the mirror face to face, "Ashes to ashes dust to dust you can no longer hurt us." We are in control of our feelings even if we think we do not. "Choices" that is what it is called. Do we choose to continue to hurt and not get help and keep our pain locked inside and let the abuser win? On the other hand, do we choose to let go and feel and cry to let the pain finally be out and be the winners ourselves? Remember, "Wages through sin pays is death and one day they will pay!"

I have come a long way and I am proud to say that a few of my alters have integrated. Pal has not integrated but Bill took her fishing. He bought her a fishing pole and we went trout fishing at Horseshoe

Lake. Of course, he thought it was his wife he took fishing but what he does not know would not hurt him. She had a great time. Sewry has integrated after saying her final good bye to Grandpa Don. The pioneer is serving God in her own way. She integrated when I began to worship God again. My mom and dad remarried August 21, 2008. In addition, the two small Cheryl's who were four years old and seven years old, integrated after they remarried. Their stories were finished. The pain had ended. Their mom and dad were back together again. Some of the alters are dormant; however, some are still very strong.

December 25, 2008, my mom called and had informed me that my dad had a major stroke and was admitted in the hospital. After several months, I guess I could not handle the fear of him dying and I switched. It was Chameleon. She called my sister and spoke with her for a while. She spoke in an Australian accent. Jane just rolled with it and helped her feel better.

He was admitted into a nursing home in Spokane and I went up to see him. When I saw him, it was very hard for me to not cry. My dad has always been an independent man and now he had to have a feeding tube and could not speak. All I could do was to hug him and tell him over and over again how much I loved him. During my visit, he got very sick and ended up in the hospital. He had pneumonia and kidney infection. He got stronger before I had to leave but I knew that this would be the last time I would ever see my Daddy again.

June 4, 2009 my Daddy passed away. Pal felt the pain of losing him during his memorial. She was all over the place. His memorial was in Richland and he had a military service. When they began playing TAPS she cried uncontrollably. My mom put her hand on my shoulder to comfort me. The Pretender was out too. She wanted everyone to think I was strong and doing just fine. When in reality I was not doing fine at all. I was falling apart missing my daddy.

As you can see, my alters stories are not resolved yet. They still have issue. It is the way I handle these issues that matter. We have to be responsible for our own actions and learn how to feel, heal, forgive and love once again and this takes hard work and determination on our part only. No one can do this for us. We are the only ones that can chose to move forward or be left behind to wallow in our own self-pity. Do we work on healing or do we stay mentally ill and get no help what so ever? The decision is up to the individual only. We cannot go through this alone.

College

Bill ended up getting hurt on the job. The injury was a head injury and was unable to work anymore. I found that finding work was becoming too difficult for me; I could not find work anywhere. Therefore, I decided I would give college one more chance. I was nervous. I have not been in school for several years and I was afraid of failure. I had so many questions going on in my mixed up head. I wanted to teach preschool age children. One question I had was, which alter is going to take the tests? On the other hand, would I be on my own. Would I be able to handle the stress of being around strangers? Shadow did not like people and I was going to be around a lot of them. I began to go to college fall quarter in 2009.

In the Early Childhood Education Program, there were classes I had to take that I found was a trigger for me switching. I remember during one of these classes (Observation, Documentation) the subject of child abuse was being discussed. My advisor knew that I had D.I.D and she was the instructor for this class and in a way that only I understood she looked at me but yet speaking to all of us that at any time we needed to leave the class to feel free to do so. I felt strong most of the time and I felt I was doing very well until Pal came out and raised her hand.

My instructor called on me and right away with one minute feeling in control and then the next my tears came rushing down my face. My hands were shaking and Pal shared what she was feeling about the subject. It was as if I could not stop her from raising my hand and saying what was on her mind. What Pal wanted to express is that children need to feel free to break their promises when they are told to not tell anyone about the abuse they are going through. It is ok to speak out to someone they feel safe with. I think she had wished she had told someone about herself a lot sooner.

Most of my classes were easy to get through until I came into a class during spring quarter (Child and Family). We had to make a display that shows what makes us who we are. Our family tree and share our family history. Pal did not hesitate on helping me make my display. There were pictures of both the good and the evil people that made me who I am today. There were pictures of my mom, sister, dad, Grandma Jones, and my Grandpa Jones. We even drew a picture that had several faces with different expressions. Looking at Grandpa's picture was one of the hardest things I had to do.

The day my project was due I had more questions. Would the other students judge me? Would I be the laughing stock of the college? Would people think I am strange and talk behind my back? Would anyone learn from me on what D.I.D was? Would I make a difference in a person's life? Would teachers and other staff members think I was incompetent or unstable in being a teacher? I was scared. However, for me to be honest with this assignment and myself I had to complete it to the best of my ability.

Everyone had his or her project up and I was shaking once again. Pal was out ready to share what had happen to her and why she was here. I showed control and was trying hard to keep my mind focused. The Pretender was out on guard to make the other students believe that I was just fine. However, in reality, I was not fine at all. Many students looked at what I was presenting and asked questions. The focus was the words

BAD MAN under my grandpa's picture and the many faces I drew. I answered their questions with strength and honesty. I survived another day. Pal was trembling but she did not cry. She kept her composure.

In this same class, another assignment was due. There were many subjects to choose from such as gay families, single families, inter cultural families, and child abuse. I chose child abuse along with three other students. My part was to tell a story about myself and the results of what child abuse did to me. Pal needed to tell her story about how Grandpa tortured her pet rooster. Once again, I was strong and then in a blink of an eye I was shaking and crying. Then I remember I switched to an alter named Courage. I regained control over myself as fast as I lost control.

I wonder why Pal needs to speak. I do not have a clue yet. One of the students I spoke to a lot about D.I.D had noticed how fast the switching happens. She told me that what she saw was one minute it was I, (Adult Cheryl) then she saw Pal then a stronger one trying to help gain control. The whole issue of child abuse was a very big trigger but I had to choose this topic. Is it for reasons of some kind of therapy? I do not know.

The first year ended successfully. I was on honor roll and made the Vice President list for good grades. Shadow helped me take tests and Courage gave me the strength to get through them. I do remember taking the tests, it is just Shadow helped me remember the answers. I am now into my second year. Once again, Pal makes her presence known. I was in my class Learning Experiences. Music and movement was the topic of conversation.

My instructor played a song called, "Christopher Robinson" that was a trigger of how Pal looked for freedom from the abuse and how she would run to the Weeping Willow tree to hide from Grandpa. I felt a strange feeling and when asked if any of these songs brought back a memory, Pal raised my hand and began to cry remembering her story of running from Grandpa. My hands were shaking out of control; I almost wanted to run out of the room.

I left the class wondering why I keep doing this to myself. It is embarrassing when I cry and shake in front of everyone. Thinking about this question, I came to realize Pal wants to be heard. She has not been able to speak her mind in years accept to me. I am in the middle of the problem and so how can I help her? I have not seen a counselor sense I was thirty years old and maybe these classes give her a reason to express herself. It is a wild guess but I think I am on to something. It is going to be interesting to see what this year's adventures are going to be.

I finished my fall quarter of 2010 with a 4.0 grade point average. This was my very first time to accomplish this. During winter quarter, I found myself not wanting to go back to school. It was getting harder for me with each class and quarter I took. I also had good news that I got a part time job working at the Colleges day care where I do my ECE lab work. So what was making me not want to go back? I discovered that I was getting afraid again that I would fail with having to work fifteen hours a week on top with keeping up with my grades. I was taking twelve credits that were four classes. I doubted myself that I could handle this school and work load. I made a choice to drop a class and this helped me be in better control over the stress I was feeling.

There were times when I fell into a deep depression and began to withdraw from people again. I get so tired of people hurting me or letting me down that I began to feel anger and hate. However, I had noticed new things about myself and that was how Shadow enjoys learning and taking in new information. Sense I am co-conscious I can see what was happening in school. I noticed that I get things done way ahead of time and can remember most of the information I studied about.

I can remember, however, while I was in high school and the first time I tried to go to college, I could not remember what I studied or worked on in school. Now how strange it feels to be in college and I can keep on track and remember my schoolwork that I have studied and have done. I found other students coming to me for help with their schoolwork and this felt strange because it is usually me asking for help instead. It felt good to be able to help others for the first time.

Winter quarter of 2011 was ending and classes were ending. My class called Learning Experiences was ending. My final class we all met in the child day care building. It was an emotional time for all of us. We have been in this class together for a year so this was the first of several goodbyes. All of us had to pick two pictures. One that represented how we felt at the beginning of Learning Experiences and one that represented how we felt at the end of Learning Experiences. One picture was a large wave coming down on top of a small boat, which I felt, represented me.

In the beginning, I felt that I was going to be swept away and lost forever. The second picture was a person riding a horse with no hands. There were some people on top of his shoulders as he rides with balance and grace. At the end of my journey in my Early Childhood Education Learning Experience I felt I had come a very long way and have built a sense of balance in my life to the point I was strong enough to help other students with their homework and trials and tribulations. It is amazing what a person can do with determination and courage. I have met some wonderful people along the way these past two years in college and I will never forget them. For the second time in my life, I received a 4.0 grade point average. I wrote a poem for this wonderful group of people it goes like this,

LEARNING EXPERIENCE CLASS OF 2011

I cannot believe it is over; our time together has nearly past. Learning Experience
2011 went by so quickly but boy did we have a blast!

Now it is not time to say goodbye but instead farewell and to remember what we
did and accomplished together so well.

Whenever we felt like giving up or that we were going to fall, we pulled together
to help each other feel ten feet tall.

As we look back on these two years together, we can see how we grew to become close
friends and weather the storm with each other, it is farewell for now
but not forever.

Now we move on to live our lives, and there will be mountains to climb but we can climb them
and get to the top; however no matter what comes our way we are strong and will never stop.

I cannot believe it is over, our time
together is nearly gone, but our memories together will
never be forgotten and continue to linger
on.

There was joy, laughter, and tears but our
class helped each other over come our fears.

We began Learning Experiences with
nervousness and uncertainty but as time together went by
we became stronger and we finished
feeling more confident and walked away
with more security.

March 18, 2011

As the 2011, winter quarter continued I noticed
friendships growing and I was inspired to write a poem
about this experience. After all, I made a promise to
myself; I would not allow anyone to get close to me
while attending Clark College. I did not care who knew
me and what other people felt about me. After all, I was
there to get an education and not to make friends.
However, friendships grew and these friends inspired
me. Here is what I wrote,

FRIEND

A friend is someone who will stand by
you through thick and thin, a friend is someone who will
stand by you until the very end.

You came into my life with no warning at
all. You made the wall I had built around me crumble
and fall.

I swore I would never let anyone in, my
heart was hard and cold, then you came along and made
it feel once again.

True friendship is so hard to find, it is our
sisterly love that makes our friendship bind.

Thank you for all the things you do, thank
you for a friendship that is so true.

May our jokes and flirts never end for
these are the things that make us laugh with no end.

A true friendship is what keeps us strong
and true; a true friendship does not just take one but
takes two.

Wherever I go in my heart, you will be.
Keep these words deep in your heart with strong
security. 4/12/2011

I found myself getting hurt and frustrated with

people and friends at the College. I began to feel hurt

when my schoolwork was not noticed nor had anyone replied to my posts. Why was this I wondered? People's opinion began to matter once again. I hated myself for this. I do not want other people's approval. I wanted to be just me, an individual who can be pleased at doing the assignments she was asked to do and be done with it. I did not want to feel I did a bad job on my schoolwork because no other student acknowledges it.

I began to hate myself for these feelings because once again I was getting involved with the people who were only in my life temporarily. People can turn on you in the blink of an eye and I let my guard down. It is not just the homework reason. However, it is for reasons that people can be kind to you one minute then angry with you the next minute for reasons that are unknown to you.

Shadow was angry that I allowed this to happen again and I had the compulsion to go back to the way I use to be at the beginning of College in 2009. I am here for an education not to make friends. I will have to find out in some way why the attention of these people became so important in the matter of just nine months long. The issue with the assignment was just the icing on the cake. These emotions come from a deeper part of me. I became to hate the schoolwork I did and resent that I wrote the words that I chose to write in my assignment. I was finding unhealthy ways of getting their attention and I know I was heading down the path of social and emotional destruction once again. This happened when I was twenty-six years old and devastation both spiritually and emotionally happened. I need to listen to Shadow and step back.

As the years went by and I was getting stronger and stronger, I began to feel like there was nothing wrong with me. The switching became less frequent and I was able to make adult decisions more often. Until one day, something happens to remind me that my struggles and the switching are not over. One evening during my spring break, I was on the phone talking to a friend when my daughter came up to me to ask if she could use something of mine for spirit day at school. I turned around and saw she had a leather vest that had Indian drawings on it that my Grandpa Jones had made and wore all the time when I was a young girl living with him. In a split second, I was coughing and began to gage and felt like I was going to throw up. Pal came out with a strong force. My friend who I was on the phone with asked if I was ok. Moreover, I explained to her what was going on and what my daughter was showing me. It was all I could do to gain my composure to not scare my little girl.

I did make her worry and I assured her that I would be ok. Pal was out to remind me that our work is far from over. I let my guard down and got caught by surprise. I was shaking and felt sick to my stomach. When I saw my daughter again after a few minutes I noticed that the vest was gone. Bill and her got rid of it. Bill hid it back into the closet. When I regained my strength back, I looked for it knowing I had to heal from this and deal with this trigger. I found it, took it out, and looked at it to let Pal know that it was just a vest and that it was not going to hurt her. I went to bed that night being Pal. She would not go back inside my mind. The next day I felt stronger but Pal was right there on the

215

surface. I am switching now as I write about this experience. This shows me that I need to stop holding Pal back and let her tell her story. I do not know yet where or when I will be able to do this.

After a while, things began to become better for me and I was no longer angry with myself for allowing myself to feel again. To feel was what I needed to do. I needed to practice becoming sociable but be strong for what I believe and feel. Soon I found myself experiencing school success that I have never known in all my life. On May 23, 2011, I was accepted and acknowledged into the Phi Theta Kappa Honor Society. This is the biggest honor society in the country. My peers came to support me and those who could not come to my induction ceremony were very encouraging. My husband, son, daughter, and Mother-in-law came to my induction ceremony as well. The same week this had happened, May 25 2011, I was given a surprise of my life. With my peers and I all grouped together during class in Learning Experience 215 Seminar, A guest speaker announced that I was the winner of the 500.00

Ronnie Johnson Scholarship award. I could not believe my ears that he actually said my name out of the thirty that was sitting around me. This just shows you that you can accomplish anything that you set your mind to with hard work and determination. If I can do this, anyone can.

Spring Quarter of 2011 was ending and I realized that all the frustration I was going through was the same frustration everyone else could be going through. There was a lot of work everyone had to do during this quarter. I learned I could not take other peoples anger and stresses personally. Some of my peers are going to be graduating and they were saddened and yet excited at the same time. Some of my peers were in pain physically and their bodies were letting them down. So sometimes, we need to step back as Shadow did and look deeper into why hurt and frustrations happen around you and it does not necessarily mean it is directed towards you. Maybe some of it is but we need to move forward and let the storm pass so to speak.

My peers in seminar ECE 215 and I began to finish preparing for out Learning Experience Graduation party and with the suggestion from one of my friends I wrote a poem for all of instructors. Certificates and roses were to be given out as well. All of us signed the poem and got frames for them. The poem went like this:

THANK YOU

We are now at the very end of our
yearlong journey, which you have seen us through, thank
you for what you do.

When we were down and full of doubt
you guided us and helped us through, thank you for what
you do.

There were times of tears and laughter,
there were times we were full of doubt, but you always
were there to see us through, thank you
for what you do.

You guided us through our doubts and
uncertainty, but rests assure you came about and gave us
strength and security.

You are our guide, mentor, and friend,
rest assure your hard work will never be forgotten not
even at our end.

You guided us through our ups and
downs; you were there through our laughter and through
our frowns.

We have been through a yearlong
journey, which you have seen us through, thank you for
what you do.

From Learning Experiences Class Of 2011

My second year of college had ended with the
whole year being a 4.0 grade point average year for me.
This was the first time that I have ever experienced this.
I for the first time in my life felt successful and good
about whom I had become and that is a person who can
accomplish anything when she set her mind to it and
someone who is not a quitter. I no longer say, "I can't" I
instead say, "Wow! Look at what I have done" and feel
proud about myself. I use to never say anything good
about myself and felt it would be wrong to do so. I never
believed anyone who would say good things about me or
to me. I never thought for one minute that feeling good
about me would, well, Feel so good. I found that I felt
more solid and less separated in my mind for the first
time I have a real good idea what being a singleton

might feel like. It took a lot for me to switch and mentally go away than before.

Then something bad began to happen. My Aunt Sue began to die of cancer and I could not stop it. I felt like Allan was dying all over again. Pal was out and so was Shadow a lot. The threat of losing another person that I love so much was more than I could bear. I was running from the fear of losing her in my mind, the switching became strong, and I no longer could find the new me. I got sick again mentally and felt so out of control in my mind. Every day I was waiting for the terrible phone call. I prayed that she would wait for me until I get to see her again August 19. The time came when I went on my trip to see my Aunt Sue. The phone call never happened and I felt like she waited for me. I took a poem I had made for her to read to her personally and this is what I wrote:

SUE

When we were down and full of doubt
you loved, guided, and helped us through. Thank you for
being you.

You guided us through our fears and
uncertainty, but rest assured you came through and gave
us strength and security. Thank you for
being you.

You are our mom, wife, sister, aunt, and
friend, be assured your hard work will never be forgotten
not even when our time ends. Thank you
for being you.

You gave us love; you gave us joy that
filled our hearts every single day. You saw us through
the sunshine and through the rainy days.
Thank you for being you.

You brought us laughter and shared in our
pain. We will never say goodbye but only say, "Until we
see you again". Thank you for being you.

We have been through a lifelong journey,
which you have seen us through, thank you for being
you.

No matter how much we need you now,
heaven needs you more. So now, it is our time to see you
through, thank you for being you.

August 02, 2011

It felt good to be able to see her again and I sat by her side telling her how much she means to me and how much I love her. My cousin Tim who was Allan's brother walked into the room. My eyes and heart lit up with such joy in seeing his beautiful smile once again. I had not seen him sense we lost our precious Allan. During this most wonderful weekend, we had some laughter and many tears.

Saturday August 20th I had a difficult time because we thought she was about to leave us and I cried so hard in her hands. One hand was in mine and the other hand was softly on my head as I sobbed telling her that it was ok to let go and that her work here on earth was done and it was time that she went to heaven to be with Allan.

Chameleon came out to speak to Aunt Sue to say thank you and to tell her how much she loved her. It felt like Chameleon had integrated but something did not feel finished yet. She was gone or hidden deep inside because of the pain of losing Aunt Sue. I have yet to see if Chameleon had truly healed, and no longer split. The

222

weekend went by too fast and before I knew it, it was time for me to say my final goodbye to my sweet precious Aunt Sue. I told her my tears were tears of love for her.

Right after my trip home from Richland, I had to go to Republic Washington to be with my other family and my daughter to support her in her horse shows. September 2nd I go that terrible call. My Aunt Sue had left us and now is resting in peace for the first time in her life that I knew of. She had always suffered in pain with her Lupus and now she is no longer suffering. Every day I feel like I am walking around in a cloud and feel unstable in my mind. At times, I feel that I can no longer handle the pain I feel inside every day.

I have one more year of college to go through so this is good for me to focus on my future because this is what my Aunt would want me to do. I began my third year in college with depression and anxiety. My first week of school was preparing to go to Aunt Sue's funeral. After coming home, I started my new job of being a lead teacher at the college day care. The stress on top of the depression was terrible. My heart was not into going to school any more. I wanted to quit and just give up. However, knowing I was so close to the finish line and seeing how far I have come I just could not stop now.

Every day was a struggle and two different times I was under so much stress that I lost my car and even forgot who I was and where I was. I switched and began wondering the parking lots looking for my car. My life felt like I was losing all control and did not know if I was going to make it through each day. I had new responsibility as a lead teacher and this pressure was very stressful. Nevertheless, I kept going and plugging along.

November 10th Bill and I were on our way to celebrate out 16-year anniversary. On the way to the beach, I received a phone call from my cousin Elisha who is my cousin Red Brian's daughter. (He was called this because of his red hair.) She had informed me that he had passed away. He was only 46 years old. There was another death in my family. I could not believe it.

So, once again I returned to school with more depression and my heart feeling heavy with grief. "One day at a time." I kept telling myself. I felt so disconnected with the rest of my family and I felt so lost and lonely.

I was switching every day and felt like if I did not do well in school this year why keep going at all. I found I was setting too high of expectations of myself. I went from knowing I was going to fail in 2009 to, I have to graduate with highest honors or I will be a failure if I do not. Last year I got the taste of success of getting straight 4.0 grade point average to maybe I will be getting a 3.9 this quarter. I was falling into depression over a B+ in one of my classes. I told myself get a grip and be proud of that and soon I did. The quarter ended and I felt successful that I made it through this one.

I called Mary Lu after all these years sense she retired and asked her to come to my graduation and she said yes. I am so excited to see her again and for her to see she had succeeded in one of her patients. I shared with her how on one day I called my mom and asked if my mom was sitting down because what I was about to tell her was a shock. My mom made it clear that yes she was sitting down. I told my mom that for the first time in my life I was going to share something that I never thought I would ever say. With tears in my eyes I told my mom I was for the first time in my whole life I was proud of myself. Yes, with hard work and determination this can happen.

Spring quarter of 2012 was the easiest quarter out of the three and I was so glade that I had a good experience with school. My journey at Clark College is about to end and it ended with pride and graduating with honors. I proved to myself that I could do this after all. I put my cap, gown on, and all of my honors ropes and my Phi Theta Kappa regalia and walked into my son's room. He looked me with a smile and said "wow!" I asked him if he was proud of me and he said yes. I told him that he could do this with hard work and determination. If I of all people can do this anyone can. It is ok to say I quit and I want to drop out, however, when you do not follow through, that is power beyond your wildest imagination. So now I can say, "I knew I could, I knew I could" instead of saying I am no good, never will be any good, never have been any good, so why try?" Failure is not an option if you are determining to succeed.

June 21st 2012 was finally here. I was about to go to my graduation. My mom, sister, children, husband, mother in law, children, and friends were all going. It was the most exciting day of my life. I was about to walk and graduate from college. One more person was there and I could not wait to see her. It was May Lu my counselor from fifteen years ago. At graduation when my name was called and I was graduating with honors I felt something that I had never felt before in my life. It was pride and honor in me.

After the ceremony, when I saw Mary Lu, I hugged her and did not want to let her go. My mom tells me that Mary Lu was so proud of me and was so pleased to see me healthy. She had never seen me this strong before. It felt so good to feel pride in myself for the first time. It also felt good to see these amazing and important people in my life so proud of me. My mom glowed with pride and this was the best feeling ever.

I will never forget my time at Clark College. August 24th 2012 was the last day at Child Family Studies. I had to say goodbye to everyone that had been such a big part of my success and education. Saying good-bye was painful and I knew what would happen, I would never see these people again. Life has a way to keep people so busy that they do not have time to visit.

My journey at Clark was over but a new one was about to begin. I had a plan that might work for me and time will tell if it does. I was going to work in the public school system and see where this will take me. In 2009 I knew what I wanted to do with my life and as I got this ECE education I began to find that there is much more for me to do somewhere else with Early Child Education. Therefore, I keep searching in hopes to find it. I need to find a place where I fit and belong. All I know it that I am stronger than I have ever been before my education, so I have succeeded in all aspects of like.

I owe a lot of my healing to my mom Ann and my sister Jane. If it were not for their support I do not know if I would have made it this far. My mom taught me the power of love and patience. Believe me when I tell you I pushed her patience to the limit. She never faltered in taking the time for me when I needed her at 1:00 am or if I needed her at 3:00 pm. She always was there for me. Sometimes to just listen to your troubled loved one without passing judgment or lecturing can mean the world in helping them open up. To get them to open up is part of the healing that they need to survive. My mom was always there for me to just listen and let me get my feelings all out.

Many years went by and an old song played on the radio from a songwriter named Stevie Nicks. The song was called "Landslide." This song was exactly how I felt for my mom. My life was built around her and she made such a positive impact on my life that I felt this song was a perfect one for only her. I made sure she knew it too. I wanted her to enjoy hearing, seeing, and feeling what I felt for her while she was still around. I did not want to wait until one day she would be gone then I would share this song with everyone else like I did with Allan. He knew I loved him but he did not know what an impact on my life that he made until it was too late for him to hear it from me. I was not about to make the same mistake with my mom. She was going to hear it straight from me how important she is in my life.

Life is too short. In a moment's instant, in a blink of an eye as it happened to Allan, they will be gone. Take the time to enjoy your loved ones and do not wait to share with them while they are around how much they mean to you and how much you dearly love them. After they are gone, there is no turning back.

I often wonder why sometimes during someone's memorial people gather around and share their stories and love with a group of people about the deceased but more times than not, they had never told the deceased loved one the depth of their love for them. I am one of them that did this very thing with Allan. All the strangers and all of the family were able to hear how much I loved him as he laid there in an open casket. He was the one that needed to hear how I felt not them but it was too late.

I also learned from my sister on how to not take crap from anyone. Nevertheless, be kind as well. I learned this too late in life by going through it the hard way. However, as they say, "Better late than never." Jane is so strong minded and yet her heart is so warm and caring as well. Therefore, I had the best of both of them. The key was to watch, learn, and apply. I could have so easily turned out a lot worse than I had but how could I with such wonderful teachers?

Then there is Mary Lu. She is the only counselor I had ever trusted. She got me through some tough stuff and helped me set a foundation to learn how to keep in control and behave myself. She taught me how to be a responsible parent to my inside family. She got through to me even if she thought she had not. I am alive today because of these three wonderful women. It is because of them and my hard work that I am able to be a devoted wife to Bill and be a good mom to my son and daughter.

My final thought: Let go, forgive and live, and learn to love again.

"Remember, yesterday cannot be changed and tomorrow has not come yet. The only day we can work with is today. If we do the best we can with today, we will not wish we had changed any yesterdays." by Ann

My story is not finished but I do have a great

start in living a normal life as closely as I can. I have come a long way but still have a long way to go. Total intergradation may never happen, however, I still can have a healthier life.

IN LOVING MEMORY, ALLAN

You touched our hearts in so many ways. You made us smile each and every day. You made our hearts feel full of life whenever you were around; the sound of your voice was a joyous sound.

Your life was cut short when helping another; you were our son, friend, father, cousin, husband, nephew, and brother. The pain we feel won't leave any time soon for the memories of you fill each and every room.

Our souls hurt and our hearts bleed, we wish for you to rest in peace. You now reside in heaven above. Rest assured you will forever be cherished and deeply loved.

Our dreams are full of thoughts of you, our tears come crashing and rushing through. Good night, our sweet dear man above, sweet dreams to our loved one that we will forever miss and love.

January 1 2007

Appendix A

My Different Personalities---My Inner Family

1. Angie---She does not think she is fat, but uses starvation as a way of punishment. Especially when very depressed and feels a lot of pain inside. 17 years old.
2. Annie---Anorexic. She thinks she is fat. Starting weight when discovered, (96 lbs) and feels that the less she weighs the better she would look.
3. Baby---She is very afraid of needles.
4. Big Anger---He is very strong. He yells and becomes very verbal. Throws outraged fits. Advances in age.
5. Big Cheryl---She is a young child who colors everything black and who lives in darkness. She thinks of death and she has not seen colorful surroundings. 7 years old. (Integrated)
6. Bitter---Not as harmful as Violet or Big

Anger. Feels betrayed. Is harsh and sarcastic. Evil look---she glares. Speaks more than Shadow does. 23 years old.

7. Canopy---Desperately looks for love in all the wrong places at any cost. 16 years old.

8. Clown---Never wants to grow up. Loves to make people laugh and does not take much very seriously. She has a carefree attitude. Advances in age.

9. Chameleon---Australian or southern accent. Can change quickly according to her surroundings.

10. Courage---He is very strong and is afraid of nothing. He has a calm way about him and has a lower voice. He is the one that may help Little Fear to be able to handle her fears.

11. Denier---She feels all this is fake to just bring attention to ourselves.

12. Executioner/Undertaker---He feels that death is a way out to put everyone's pain to an end. However, his new job now is to bury the bad memories. Advances in age.

13. Little Anger---Mama's girl. She likes to show and tell about the pain she feels inside by cutting on herself. She is most comforted by her teddy bear. 2 years.

14. Little Fear---She has a childlike voice and is the one who is deathly afraid of needles and maybe some other things. Her story is of a abusive babysitter. 3 years old.

15. Little Cheryl---Daddy's girl---4 years old (Integrated)

16. No Name---Friendly and very active and wants to do things. A good housekeeper. Protects the body from depression.

17. Pal---The Interpreter. She will speak for someone who cannot or will not speak for themselves. 8 years old at first, then grew to be 11 years old. She is afraid to go to religious meetings because Grandpa said that his games were ok with God.

18. Quiet One---Is very scared of people. She is jumpy and sits in a curled up ball and rocks. She will not speak. 10 years old.

19. Sewry---She loves Papa (Jack, an Elder in the congregation) She denies that Grandpa Don is dead and she is afraid of Grandpa Jones. Does not believe he is dead. 13 years old. (Integrated)

20. Shadow---She does not trust anyone because people have been hurtful. She studies people and her facial features are very stern looking and have a glare look about her. She wears her makeup very thick to hide her identity.

21. **Lynn---The core personality. 26 years old, when it was discovered she had M.P.D She ages with the body.**

22. The Peace Maker---Her purpose is to help Pal and the other little ones feel safe. She is to help everyone understand that God had nothing to with the abuse.

23. The pioneer----She is the one who feels that she is still one of Gods people. She is mad that she was removed from the Christian congregation for something she did not do. She feels that no one cares for her. 21 years

old. (Integrated)

24. The Pretender---Pretends that she is fine when she is scared or afraid of someone's anger or of stressful issues.

25. There is an older Cheryl that is 12 years old. She loves to play with the German Shepard that she grew up with and who was her best friend. I remember her playing with the dog in the back yard.

26. Violet---She is very violent and inflicts pain as a way of punishment. At times hates men and the body. Teenager.

Walking out of the darkness, Stepping into the light,

With hard work and courage, you can see your future that can be so bright.

Do not give up nor ever give in, you can see you true beauty that is deep within.

References

MDWeb, *better information, better health*, Web MD, LLC

Watchtower Bible Tract Society, Brooklyn New York

Buzzle.com by, Nilesh Parekh

Web MD, http://www.webmd.com/mental-health/dissociative-identity-disorder-multiple-personality-disorder

www.ingramcontent.com/pod-product-compliance
Lightning Source LLC
Chambersburg PA
CBHW070352290526
45790CB00004B/1460